Post-Democracy

Titles in this series

Post-Democracy

COLIN CROUCH

polity

First published in 2004 by Polity Press Ltd.

Reprinted 2005, 2007, 2008 (three times), 2009 (twice), 2010 (twice), 2011 (four times),
2012 (twice), 2013, 2014 (twice), 2015 (twice), 2016 (twice), 2017, 2018, 2019, 2020

Polity Press
65 Bridge Street
Cambridge CB2 1UR, UK

Polity Press
350 Main Street
Malden, MA 02148, USA

A catalogue record for this book is available from the British Library.

Library of Congress Cataloging-in-Publication Data

Crouch, Colin, 1944–
    Post-democracy / Colin Crouch.
       p. cm.—(Themes for the 21st century)
Includes bibliographical references and index.
    ISBN 978–0–7456–3314–5
    ISBN 978–0–7456–3315–2 (pb)
1. Democracy. 2. Globalization. 3. Political participation.
4. Social classes. 5. Elite (Social sciences) I. Title. II. Series.

    JC423.C767 2004
    321.8–dc22

                                                        2003021910

Typeset in 10.5 on 12 pt Plantin
by Kolam Information Services Pvt. Ltd, Pondicherry, India.

Printed and bound in the United States of America by LSC Communications

For further information on Polity, visit our website:
www.polity.co.uk

Contents

Preface

Troubled thoughts of various kinds gradually came together to form this book. By the late 1990s it was becoming clear in most of the industrialized world that, whatever
the party identity of the government, there was steady,
consistent pressure for state policy to favour the interests
of the wealthy – those who benefited from the unrestricted
operation of the capitalist economy rather than those who
needed some protection from it. What seemed to be the
extraordinary opportunity presented by the fact that nearly
all member states of the European Union were dominated
by centre-left parties was resulting in no notable achievements at all. As a sociologist, I could not be content with
explanations of this that concentrated on the venality of
politicians. It was related to structural forces: nothing was
emerging within the body politic to replace the challenge
to the interests of the wealthy and socially advantaged that
had been presented for most of the twentieth century by
the organized manual working class. The numerical decline of that class was returning politics to something
resembling what it always had been before: something to
serve the interests of various sections of the privileged.

Around that time, Andrew Gamble and Tony Wright
asked me to contribute a chapter to the book that they
were preparing for *The Political Quarterly* and the Fabian

Society on 'the new social democracy'. I therefore developed these gloomy thoughts into a discussion of 'The Parabola of Working Class Politics' (A. Gamble and T. Wright (eds) _The New Social Democracy_ [Oxford: Blackwell, 1999], pp. 69–83). Chapter 3 of the current volume is an extended version of this chapter.

Like many others during the late 1990s, I was also becoming uncomfortable with the character of a new political class that was emerging around the New Labour government in the United Kingdom. The various circles of party leadership seemed to be being replaced by an overlapping network of advisers, consultants and lobbyists of various kinds, mainly for corporations seeking favours from government. The phenomenon was by no means limited to New Labour or to the UK, but was perhaps to be seen most sharply there because the old leading circles of the Labour Party had become so discredited during the early 1980s that they were particularly easy to bypass.

I had learned much from Alessandro Pizzorno about the fine structure of political life and its relations to the rest of society, and when I was asked by Donatella Della Porta, Margaret Greco and Arpad Szakolczai to contribute to a _Festschrift_ that they were organizing for Sandro, I took the opportunity to develop these thoughts more rigorously. The resulting essay, 'Intorno ai partiti e ai movimenti: militanti, iscritti, professionisti e il mercato' (D. Della Porta, M. Greco and A. Szakolczai (eds), _Identità, riconoscimento, scambio: Saggi in onore di Alessandro Pizzorno_ [Rome: Laterza, 2000], pp. 135–50), in modified form, is included here as chapter 4 of the present volume.

These two different themes – the vacuum left in mass political participation by the decline of the working class, and the growth of a political class linked to the rest of society more or less solely via business lobbyists – were clearly connected. They also helped account for what an increasing number of observers were coming to perceive as worrying signs of weakness in western democracies. We were possibly entering a period of *post-democracy*. I then approached the Fabian Society to see if they would be interested in a general discussion of this phenomenon. I developed the concept of post-democracy, added a discussion of what seemed to me to be a key institution behind the changes (the global firm), and some ideas for how concerned citizens should respond to the predicament (shorter versions of chapters 1, 2 and 6). This was published as *Coping with Post-Democracy* (Fabian Ideas 598, London: The Fabian Society, 2000).

This little work attracted some attention, and came to the notice of Giuseppe Laterza and his eponymous publishing firm. He was interested in producing an Italian version of the work within his series of short books on key social and political issues, but pointed out to me that the existing work was heavily geared to a British readership. I therefore set about providing a wider European base for the empirical discussions in the book *Postdemocrazia* (Rome: Laterza, 2003).

While I was engaged on this task I was becoming interested in a new topic: the commercialization of education and other public services that was taking place in the UK and many other countries. My wife was at that point working as a senior education officer in a British shire county. I observed the pressures being increasingly placed by central government on her and her colleagues throughout the country to offer aspects of their work and that of schools to private firms, and to change the way in which public education services were conceived and structured so that they could easily be transferred to such firms – indeed, so that they would be more logically operated by firms than by public authorities. Similar developments were taking place in the health service and other parts of the welfare state. This seemed to raise major issues of the idea of citizenship in the welfare state. I examined both the general questions involved and the facts of the particular case of education in another Fabian Society publication: *Commercialization or Citizenship: Education Policy and the Future of Public Services* (Fabian Ideas 606, London: The Fabian Society, 2003).

But, while being part of the debate over the future of the welfare state, these issues were also relevant to discussions of problems of democracy. The rising political importance of the global firm, the vacuum left by the decline of the working class, and the way in which a new political class of political advisers and business lobbyists was filling that vacuum all helped explain why government social policy was becoming increasingly obsessed with giving work to private contractors. This debate was also part of the post-democracy debate, and in fact provided a major example of the practical consequences of post-democracy. I therefore integrated the main general arguments from *Commercialization or Citizenship* into the text of *Postdemocrazia*.

The opportunity then appeared to have this now considerably expanded version of *Coping with Post-Democracy* published in English again, through Polity, incorporating a few further changes helpfully suggested by the publisher's referees, and by the debate stimulated by the Italian edition. Some commentators, including Giuliano Amato and Michele Salvati, said that I was talking about problems for social democracy rather than democracy in general. Ralf Dahrendorf made a similar point, saying that I was insisting on equalitarian rather than liberal democracy. I would contest these arguments. In polities with universal citizenship there are problems for all forms of serious, principled politics if vast, socially defined groups within the electorate become detached from engagement in public life and passively allow their marginal political involvement to be shaped by small elites. Neo-liberals in particular should be just as concerned as social democrats if the economic actions of government become distorted by lobbies with privileged political access entering the vacuum which this passivity leaves, corrupting the markets in which they believe.

1

Why Post-Democracy?

The early twenty-first century sees democracy at a highly paradoxical moment. At one level it could be said to be enjoying a world-historical peak. The past quarter-century has seen first the Iberian peninsula, then most dramatically large parts of the former Soviet empire, South Africa, South Korea and some other parts of South-East Asia, and finally some countries of Latin America adopt at least the important form of more or less free and fair elections. More nation states are currently accepting democratic arrangements of this kind than at any previous time. According to the findings of a research project on global democracy led by Philippe Schmitter, the number of countries holding reasonably free elections grew from 147 in 1988 (the eve of the collapse of the Soviet system) to 164 by 1995, and 191 in 1999 (Schmitter, private communication, October 2002; see also Schmitter and Brouwer 1999). On a stricter definition of full and free elections, the findings are more ambiguous: an actual decline from 65 to 43 between 1988 and 1995, but then a climb to 88 cases.

Meanwhile, however, in the established democracies of Western Europe, Japan, the United States of America and other parts of the industrialized world, where more subtle indicators of its health should be used, matters are less optimistic.

One need point only to the US presidential elections of 2000, where there was almost irrefutable evidence of serious ballot-rigging in Florida, a result which was decisive to the victory of George W. Bush, the brother of the state's governor. Apart from some demonstrations among Black Americans, there were very few expressions of outrage at tampering with the democratic process. The prevailing mood seemed to be that achieving an outcome – any outcome – was important in order to restore confidence to the stock markets, and that was more important than ensuring that the verdict of the majority was truly discovered.

Less anecdotally, a recent report for the Trilateral Commission – an elite body which brings together scholars from Western Europe, Japan and the USA – concluded that all was not well with democracy in these countries (Pharr and Putnam 2000). The authors saw the problem primarily in terms of a declining capacity of politicians to act because their legitimacy was increasingly in doubt. This rather elitist position did not lead them to see that the public might also have a problem, possessing politicians whom it finds it hard to trust; however, their conclusions are disturbing enough. Of course, as Putnam, Pharr and Dalton (2000) pointed out, one can interpret growing public dissatisfaction with politics and politicians as evidence of the health of democracy: politically mature, demanding publics expect more from their leaders than did their deferential predecessors of a previous generation. We shall return to this important caution at a number of points.

Democracy thrives when there are major opportunities for the mass of ordinary people actively to participate, through discussion and autonomous organizations, in shaping the agenda of public life, and when they are actively using these opportunities. This is ambitious in expecting very large numbers of people to participate in a lively way in serious political discussion and in framing the agenda, rather than be the passive respondents to opinion polls, and to be knowledgeably engaged in following political events and issues. It is an ideal model, which can almost never be fully achieved, but, like all impossible ideals, it sets a marker. It is always valuable and intensely practical to consider where our conduct stands in relation to an ideal, since in that way we can try to improve. It is essential to take this approach to democracy rather than the more common one, which is to scale down definitions of the ideal so that they conform to what we easily achieve. That way lies complacency, self-congratulation and an absence of concern to identify ways in which democracy is being weakened.

One recalls the writings of US political scientists in the 1950s and early 1960s, who would adapt their definition of democracy so that it corresponded to actual practice in the USA and Britain rather than accept any defects in the political arrangements of those two countries (e.g. Almond and Verba 1963). This was Cold War ideology rather than scientific analysis. A similar approach is dominating contemporary thinking. Again under US influence, democracy is increasingly being defined as *liberal* democracy: an historically contingent form, not a normative last word (see the critical accounts of this in Dahl 1989 and Schmitter 2002). This is a form that stresses electoral participation as the main type of mass participation, extensive freedom for lobbying activities, which mainly means business lobbies, and a form of polity that avoids interfering with a capitalist economy. It is a model that has little interest in widespread citizen involvement or the role of organizations outside the business sector.

Satisfaction with the unambitious democratic expectations of liberal democracy produces complacency about the rise of what I call post-democracy. Under this model, while elections certainly exist and can change governments, public electoral debate is a tightly controlled spectacle, managed by rival teams of professionals expert in the techniques of persuasion, and considering a small range of issues selected by those teams. The mass of citizens plays a passive, quiescent, even apathetic part, responding only to the signals given them. Behind this spectacle of the electoral game, politics is really shaped in private by interaction between elected governments and elites that overwhelmingly represent business interests. This model, like the maximal ideal, is also an exaggeration, but enough elements of it are recognizable in contemporary politics to make it worth while asking where our political life stands on a scale running between it and the maximal democratic model; and in particular to appraise in which direction it seems to be moving between them. It is my contention that we are increasingly moving towards the post-democratic pole.

If I am right about this, the factors which I shall identify as causing the movement also help explain something else, of particular concern to the social democrats and others concerned for political egalitarianism for whom this book is principally intended. Under the conditions of a post-democracy that increasingly cedes power to business lobbies, there is little hope for an agenda of strong egalitarian policies for the redistribution of power and wealth, or for the restraint of powerful interests.

Further, if politics is becoming post-democratic in this sense, then the political left will be experiencing a transformation that seems to reverse most of its achievements during the twentieth century. During this period the left struggled, at some times and in some places with gradual and mainly peaceful progress, in other times and places against violence and repression, to admit the voices of ordinary people into affairs of state. Are these voices now being squeezed out again, as the economically powerful continue to use their instruments of influence while those of the *demos* become weakened? This would not mean a return full circle to conditions of the early twentieth century, because, as well as moving in the opposite direction, we are located at a different point in historical time and carry the inheritance of our recent past with us. Rather, democracy has moved in a parabola. If you trace the outline of a parabola, your pen passes one of the co-ordinates twice: going in towards the centre of the parabola, and then again at a different point on the way out. This image will be important to much of what I have to say below about the complex characteristics of post-democracy.

Elsewhere (Crouch 1999b), as noted in the preface, I have written about 'the parabola of working-class politics', concentrating on the experience of the British working class. I had in mind how, during the course of the twentieth century, that class moved from being a weak, excluded, but increasingly numerous and strong force banging on the door of political life; through having its brief moment at the centre, in the period of formation of the welfare state, Keynesian demand management and institutionalized industrial relations; to end as a numerically declining and increasingly disorganized grouping being marginalized within that life as the achievements of the mid-century were booted out after it. The parabola can be seen most clearly in the British case, and perhaps also that of Australia: the rise of working-class political power there was gradual and extensive; its decline has been particularly steep. In other countries where the rise was similarly gradual and extended – primarily in Scandinavia – the decline has been far less. The North American working class had less impressive achievements before an even more profound decline set in. With some exceptions (e.g. the

Netherlands, Switzerland), in most of Western Europe and in Japan the earlier history was more disturbed and punctuated with violence. The countries of Central and Eastern Europe have had a very different trajectory caused by the distorted and corrupted shape imposed by the capture of working-class movements by communism.

The decline of the manual working class is only one, important, aspect of the parabolic experience of democracy itself. The two issues, the crisis of egalitarian politics and the trivialization of democracy, are not necessarily the same. Egalitarians might say that they do not care how manipulative of democracy a government is, provided it divides society's wealth and power more evenly. A conservative democrat will point out that improving the quality of political debate need not necessarily result in more redistributive policies. But at certain crucial points the two issues do intersect, and it is on this intersection that I intend to focus. My central contentions are that, while the forms of democracy remain fully in place – and today in some respects are actually strengthened – politics and government are increasingly slipping back into the control of privileged elites in the manner characteristic of pre-democratic times; and that one major consequence of this process is the growing impotence of egalitarian causes. One implication of this is that to view the ills of democracy as just the fault of the mass media and the rise of spin-doctors is to miss some far more profound processes that are currently at work.

The democratic moment

Societies probably come closest to democracy in my maximal sense in the early years of achieving it or after great regime crises, when enthusiasm for democracy is wide-spread; when many diverse groups and organizations of ordinary people share in the task of trying to frame a political agenda which will at last respond to their concerns; when the powerful interests which dominate undemocratic societies are wrong-footed and thrown on the defensive; and when the political system has not quite discovered how to manage and manipulate the new demands. Popular political movements and parties themselves may well be dominated by boss figures whose personal style is anything but democratic; but they are at least subject to lively active pressure from a mass movement which itself in turn represents something of the aspirations of ordinary people.

In most of Western Europe and North America we had our democratic moment around the mid-point of the twentieth century: slightly before the Second World War in North America and Scandinavia; soon after it for many others. By then, not only had the final great movements of resistance against democracy – fascism and Nazism – been defeated in a global war, but also political change moved in tandem with a major economic development which made possible the realization of many democratic goals. For the first time in the history of capitalism, the general health of the economy was seen as depending on the prosperity of the mass of wage-earning people. This was clearly expressed in the economic policies associated with Keynesianism, but also in the logic of the cycle of mass production and mass consumption embodied in so-called 'Fordist' production methods. In those industrial societies which did not become communist, a certain social compromise was reached between capitalist business interests and working people. In exchange for the survival of the capitalist system and the general quietening of protest against the inequalities it produced, business interests learned to accept certain limitations on their capacity to use their power. And democratic political capacity concentrated at the level of the nation state was able to guarantee those limitations, as firms were largely subordinate to the authority of national states.

This pattern of development was seen in its purest form in Scandinavia, the Netherlands and the UK. Elsewhere there were important differences. Although the USA started alongside Scandinavia with major welfare reforms in the 1930s, the general weakness of the labour movement in that country led to a gradual attrition of its early advances in welfare policy and industrial relations during the 1950s, though it remained broadly Keynesian in economic policy approach until the 1980s; the essential democracy of the mass-production, mass-consumption US economy has continued to reproduce itself. The West German state, in contrast, did not embark on Keynesian demand management until the late 1960s, but did have very strongly institutionalized industrial relations and, eventually, a strong welfare state. In France and Italy the process was less clear. There was an ambiguous combination of concessions to working-class demands to weaken the attractions of communism combined with rejection of direct representation of workers' interests, partly because these were predominantly borne by communist parties and unions. Spain and Portugal did not enter the democratic period at all until the 1970s, just when the conditions which had prolonged the post-war model were coming to an end; and Greek democracy was interrupted by civil war and several years of military dictatorship.

The high level of widespread political involvement of the late 1940s and early 1950s was partly a result of the intensely important and public task of post-war reconstruction, and in a few countries also a residue of the intensified public character of life during war itself. As such it could not be expected to be sustained for many years. Elites soon learned how to manage and manipulate. People became disillusioned, bored or preoccupied with the business of everyday life. The growing complexity of issues after the major initial achievements of reform made it increasingly difficult to take up informed positions, to make intelligent comment, or even to know what 'side' one was on. Participation in political organizations declined almost everywhere, and eventually even the minimal act of voting was beset by apathy. Nevertheless, the basic democratic imperatives of an economy dependent on the cycle of mass production and mass consumption sustained by public spending remained the main policy impetus of the mid-century moment until the mid-1970s.

The oil crises of that decade tested to destruction the capacity of the Keynesian system to manage inflation. The rise of the service economy reduced the role played by manual workers in sustaining the production/consumption cycle. The effect of this was considerably delayed in West Germany, Austria, Japan and, to some extent, Italy, where manufacturing continued to thrive and to employ growing numbers longer than elsewhere. And matters were very considerably different in Spain, Portugal and Greece, where the working classes were just beginning to enjoy the kind of political influence that their northern cousins had known for several decades. This ushered in the brief period when social democracy seemed to take a summer holiday: the Baltic Scandinavian countries which had long been its stronghold moved to the political right, while parties of the left became significant in governments in several Mediterranean countries. But the interlude was brief. Although these southern governments did have considerable achievements in expanding the previously minimal welfare states of their countries (Maravall 1997), social democracy never became deeply embedded.

The working class did not acquire the kind of strength that had been possible elsewhere during the high tide of industrialism.

Worse still, in Italy, Greece and Spain these governments became enmeshed in scandals of political corruption. By the late 1990s it had become clear that corruption was by no means limited to parties of the left or to countries of the south, but had become a widespread feature of political life (Della Porta 2000; Della Porta and Mény 1995; Della Porta and Vannucci 1999). Indeed, corruption is a powerful indicator of the poor health of democracy, as it signals a political class which has become cynical, amoral and cut off from scrutiny and from the public. A sad initial lesson demonstrated by the southern European cases, and soon after repeated in Belgium, France and then occasionally in Germany and the United Kingdom, was that parties of the left were by no means immune to a phenomenon which should have been anathema to their movements and parties.

By the late 1980s the global deregulation of financial markets had shifted the emphasis of economic dynamism away from mass consumption and on to stock exchanges. First in the USA and the UK, but soon spreading in eager imitation, the maximization of shareholder value became the main indicator of economic success (Dore 2000); debates about a wider stakeholder economy went very quiet. Everywhere the share in income taken by labour as opposed to capital, which had risen steadily for decades, began to decline again. The democratic economy had been tamed alongside the democratic polity. The USA continued to enjoy its reputation as the global exemplar of democracy, and by the early 1990s became again, as during the post-war period, the unquestioned model for everyone seeking to be associated with dynamism and modernity. However, the social model now presented by the USA was very different from what it had been in the earlier period. Then, for most Europeans and the Japanese it represented a creative compromise between a vigorous capitalism and highly wealthy elites, on the one hand, and egalitarian values, strong trade unions, and the welfare policies of the New Deal, on the other. European conservatives had largely believed that there was no space for a positive-sum exchange between them and the masses, a belief which led many of them to support fascist and Nazi oppression and terror in the inter-war period. When those approaches to the popular challenge collapsed in war and ignominy, they had reached eagerly for the American compromise based on the mass-production economy. It is in this way as much as in its military achievements during the war that the USA established a legitimate claim to be the world's principal champion of democracy.

However, during the Reagan years the USA changed fundamentally. Its welfare provision had become residual, its unions marginalized, and its divisions between rich and poor had started to resemble those of Third World countries, reversing the normal historical association between modernization and the reduction of inequalities. This was a US example which elites throughout the world, including those in countries emerging from communism, could embrace with open arms. At the same time US concepts of democracy increasingly equated it with limited government within an unrestrained capitalist economy and reduced the democratic component to the holding of elections.

· Democratic crisis? What crisis?

Given the difficulty of sustaining anything approaching maximal democracy, declines from democratic moments must be accepted as inevitable, barring major new moments of crisis and change which permit a new re-engagement – or, more realistically in a society in which universal suffrage has been achieved, the emergence of new identities within the existing framework which change the shape of popular participation. As we shall see, these possibilities do occur, and are important. For much of the time, however, we must expect an entropy of democracy. It then becomes important to understand the forces at work within this and to adjust our approach to political participation to it. Egalitarians cannot reverse the arrival of post-democracy, but we must learn to cope with it – softening, amending, sometimes challenging it – rather than simply accepting it.

In the following discussion I try to explore some of the deeper causes of the phenomenon, and then ask what we can do about it. First, however, we must look in more detail at doubts which many will still entertain at my initial statement that all is not well with the state of our democracy.

It can be argued that democracy is currently enjoying one of its most splendid periods. Not only have there been the major extensions of elected government referred to at the outset, but closer to home, within the so-called 'advanced countries', it can clearly be argued that politicians receive less deference and uncritical respect from the public and mass media than perhaps ever before. Government and its secrets are increasingly laid bare to the democratic gaze. There are insistent and often success-ful calls for more open government and for constitutional reforms to make governments more responsible to the people. Surely, we today live in a *more* democratic age than in any 'democratic moment' of the third quarter of the twentieth century? Politicians were then trusted and respected by naïve and deferential voters in a way that they did not deserve. What seems from one perspective to be manipulation of opinion by today's politicians can be viewed from another as politicians so worried about the views of a subtle and complex electorate that they have to devote enormous resources to discovering what it thinks, and then respond anxiously to it. Surely it is an advance in democratic quality that politicians are today more afraid than were their predecessors to shape the political agenda, preferring to take much of it from the findings of market research techniques and opinion polls?

This optimistic view of current democracy has nothing to say about the fundamental problem of the power of corporate elites. This is the theme at the centre of concern in the following chapters of this book. But there is also an important difference between two concepts of the active democratic citizen, which is not recognized in optimistic discussions. On the one hand is positive citizenship, where groups and organizations of people together develop collective identities, perceive the interests of these identities, and autonomously formulate demands based on them, which they pass on to the political system. On the other hand is the negative activism of blame and complaint, where the main aim of political controversy is to see politicians called to account, their heads placed on blocks, and their public and private integrity held up to intimate scrutiny. This difference is closely paralleled by two different conceptions of citizens' rights. Positive rights stress citizens' abilities to participate in their polity: the right to vote, to form and join organizations, to receive accurate information. Negative rights are those which protect the individual against others, especially against the state: rights to sue, rights to property.

Democracy needs both of these approaches to citizenship, but at the present time the negative is receiving considerably more emphasis. This is worrying, because it is obviously positive citizenship that represents democracy's creative energies. The negative model, for all its aggression against the political class, shares with the passive approach to democracy the idea that politics is essentially an affair of elites, who are then subjected to blaming and shaming by an angry populace of spectators when we discover that they got something wrong. Paradoxically, every time that we regard a failure or disaster as being somehow resolved when a hapless minister or official is forced to resign, we connive at a model which regards government and politics as the business of small groups of elite decision-makers alone.

Finally, one might question the strength of the moves towards 'open government', transparency and openness to investigation and criticism which can otherwise be seen as the contribution to the general political good that neo-liberalism has made since the last quarter of the twentieth century, since these moves are currently being countered by measures for tightened state security and secrecy. These follow a number of developments. In many countries there has been a perceived rise in crime and violence, and anxiety about the immigration of people from poor countries into the rich world and about foreigners in general. These all achieved a symbolic climax in the murderous and suicidal air crashes engineered by Islamic terrorists in the USA on 11 September 2001. Since then, in the USA and Europe alike, there have been, on the one hand, new justifications for state secrecy and the refusal of rights to scrutinize state activities, and, on the other, new rights for states to spy on their populations and invade recently won rights of privacy. It is likely that in coming years many of the gains in government transparency of the 1980s and 1990s will be reversed, apart from those which are of primary interest to global financial interests.

Alternatives to electoral politics

Different evidence to contest my claim that democracy is weakening comes from the lively world of causes and pressure groups which are growing in importance. Do these not constitute the embodiment of a healthy positive citizenship? There is a danger that one might concentrate too much on politics in the narrow sense of party and electoral struggle, and ignore the displacement of creative citizenship away from this arena to the wider one of cause groups. Organizations on behalf of human rights, the homeless, the Third World, the environment and many other causes could be said to provide a far richer democracy, because they enable us to choose highly specific causes, whereas working through a party requires us to accept a whole package. Further, the range of objects of action available becomes far more extensive than just helping politicians get elected. And modern means of communication like the Internet make it ever easier and cheaper to organize and co-ordinate new cause groups.

This is a very powerful argument. I do not fully dissent from it, and as we shall see in the final chapter, within it lie some of the answers to our present predicament. However, it also embodies some weaknesses. We need first to distinguish between those cause activities that pursue an essentially political agenda, seeking to secure action or legislation or spending by public authorities, and those that tackle tasks directly and ignore politics. (Of course, some groups in the former category may also do the latter, but that is not the issue here.)

Cause groups that set their face against political engagement have grown considerably in recent times. This is partly itself a reflection of the malaise of democracy and widespread cynicism about its capacities. This is particularly the case in the USA, where left-wing disgust at the monopolization of politics by big business interests joins right-wing rejection of big government to celebrate non-political civic virtue. One notes here the extraordinary popularity among US liberals of Robert Putnam's book on civil society *Making Democracy Work* (Putnam, with Leonardi and Nanetti, 1993). This presents a rather idealized account of the way in which in many parts of Italy strong norms and practices of community co-operation and trust have developed without reference to the state. Italian critics have pointed out that Putnam ignores the fundamental role of *local* politics in sustaining this model (Bagnasco 1999; Piselli 1999; Trigilia 1999).

In the UK too there has been a major and highly diverse growth of self-help groups, communitarian networks, neighbourhood watch schemes and charitable activities trying desperately to fill the gaps in care left by a retreating welfare state. Most of these developments are interesting, valuable, worthy. However, precisely because they involve turning away from politics, they cannot be cited as indicators of the health of democracy, which is by definition political. Indeed, some such activities can flourish in non-democratic societies, where political involvement is either dangerous or impossible, and where the state is particularly likely to be indifferent to social problems.

More complex are the second type of cause organizations: politically oriented campaigns and lobbies which, though not seeking to influence or organize votes, do work directly to affect government policy. Vitality of this kind is evidence of a strong *liberal* society; but this is not the same as a strong *democracy*. Since we have become so accustomed to the joint idea of liberal democracy we tend today not to see that there are two separate elements at work. Democracy requires certain rough equalities in a real capacity to affect political outcomes by all citizens. Liberalism requires free, diverse and ample opportunities to affect those outcomes. These are related and mutually dependent conditions. Maximal democracy certainly cannot flourish without strong liberalism. But the two are different things, and at points even conflict.

The difference was well understood in nineteenth-century bourgeois liberal circles, who were acutely aware of a tension: the more that there was insistence on the criterion of equality of political capacity, the more likely was it that rules and restrictions would be developed to reduce inequalities, threatening liberalism's insistence on free and multiple means of action.

Take a simple and important example. If no restrictions are placed on the funds which parties and their friends may use to promote their cause and on the kinds of media resources and advertising which may be purchased, then parties favoured by wealthy interests will have major advantages in winning elections. Such a regime favours liberalism but hinders democracy, because there is nothing like a level playing field of competition as required by the equality criterion. This is the case with US politics. In contrast, state funding for parties, restrictions of spending on campaigns, rules about buying time on television for political purposes, help ensure rough equality and there-fore assist democracy, but at the expense of curtailing liberty.

The world of politically active causes, movements and lobbies belongs to liberal rather than to democratic polit-ics, in that few rules govern the modalities for trying to exercise influence. The resources available to different causes vary massively and systematically. Lobbies on behalf of business interests always have an enormous advantage, for two separate reasons. First, as argued convincingly by Lindblom (1977), a disillusioned former celebrator of the US model of pluralism, business interests are able to threaten that, unless government listens to them, their sector will not be successful, which will in turn jeopardize government's own core concern with economic success. Second, they can wield enormous funds for their lobbying, not just because they are rich to start with, but because success of the lobbying will bring increased profits to the business: the lobbying costs constitute investment. Non-business interests can rarely claim anything so potent as damage to economic success; and success of their lobbying will not bring material reward (this is true by definition of a non-business interest), so their costs represent expenditure, not investment.

Those who argue that they can work best for, say, healthy food, by setting up a cause group to lobby government and ignore electoral politics, must remember that the food and chemicals industries will bring battleships against their rowing boats. A flourishing liberalism certainly enables all manner of causes, good and bad, to seek political influence, and makes possible a rich array of public participation in politics. But unless it is balanced by healthy democracy in the strict sense it will always proceed in a systematically distorted way. Of course, electoral party politics is also disfigured by the inequalities of funding produced by the role of business interests. But the extent to which this is true depends on how much of liberalism is permitted to leak into democracy. The more that a level playing field is ensured in such matters as party funding and media access, the more true the democracy. On the other hand, the more that the modalities of liberal politicking flourish while electoral democracy atrophies, the more vulnerable the latter becomes to distorting inequalities, and the weaker the democratic quality of the polity. A lively world of cause groups is evidence that we have the potential to come closer to maximal democracy.

But this cannot be fully evaluated until we examine what use post-democratic forces are also making of the opportunities of liberal society.

Similar arguments can be used to refute a further US neo-liberal argument that modern citizens no longer need the state as much as their predecessors did; that they are more self-reliant and more able and willing to achieve their goals through the market economy; and that therefore it is reasonable that they should be less concerned about political matters (for example, see Hardin 2000). But corporate lobbies show no signs of losing interest in using the state to achieve favours for themselves. As the current situation in the USA shows, these lobbies cluster at least as thickly around a non-interventionist, neo-liberal state with low public spending levels as around high-spending welfare states. *Indeed, the more that the state withdraws from providing for the lives of ordinary people, making them apathetic about politics, the more easily can corporate interests use it more or less unobserved as their private milch-cow.* Failure to recognize this is the fundamental naïveté of neo-liberal thought.

The symptoms of post-democracy

If we have only two concepts – democracy and non-democracy – we cannot take discussion about the health of democracy very far. The idea of post-democracy helps us describe situations when boredom, frustration and disillusion have settled in after a democratic moment; when powerful minority interests have become far more active than the mass of ordinary people in making the political system work for them; where political elites have learned to manage and manipulate popular demands; where people have to be persuaded to vote by top-down publicity campaigns. This is not the same as non-democracy, but describes a period in which we have, as it were, come out the other side of the parabola of democracy. There are many symptoms that this is occurring in contemporary advanced societies, constituting evidence that we are indeed moving further away from the maximal ideal of democracy towards the post-democratic model. To pursue this further we must look briefly at the use of 'post-' terms in general.

The idea of 'post-' is thrown around rather easily in contemporary debate: post-industrial, post-modern, post-liberal, post-ironic. However, it can mean something very precise. Essential is the idea mentioned above of an historical parabola through which the thing being attached to the 'post-' prefix can be seen as moving. This will be true whatever one is talking about, so let us first talk abstractly about 'post-X'. Time period 1 is pre-X, and will have certain characteristics associated with lack of X. Time period 2 is the high tide of X, when many things are touched by it and changed from their state in time 1. Time period 3 is post-X. This implies that something new has come into existence to reduce the importance of X by going beyond it in some sense; some things will therefore look different from both time 1 and time 2. However, X will still have left its mark; there will be strong traces of it still around; while some things start to look rather like they did in time 1 again. 'Post-' periods should therefore be expected to be very complex. (If the above seems too abstract, the reader can try replacing 'X' by 'industrial' every time it occurs, to have the point illustrated with a very prominent example.)

Post-democracy can be understood in this way. At one level the changes associated with it give us a move *beyond* democracy to a form of political responsiveness more flexible than the confrontations that produced the ponderous compromises of the mid-century years. To some extent we have gone beyond the idea of rule by the people to challenge the idea of rule at all. This is reflected in the shifting balance within citizenship referred to above: the collapse of deference to government, and in particular in the treatment of politics by the mass media; the insistence on total openness by government; and the reduction of politicians to something more resembling shopkeepers than rulers, anxiously seeking to discover what their 'customers' want in order to stay in business.

The political world then makes its own response to the unattractive and subservient position in which these changes threaten to place it. Unable to return to earlier positions of authority and respect, unable to discern easily what demands are coming to it from the population, it has recourse to the well-known techniques of contemporary political manipulation, which give it all the advantages of discovering the public's views without the latter being able to take control of the process for itself. It also imitates the methods of other worlds that have a more certain and self-confident sense of themselves: show business and the marketing of goods.

From this emerge the familiar paradoxes of contemporary politics: both the techniques for manipulating public opinion and the mechanisms for opening politics to scrutiny become ever more sophisticated, while the content of party programmes and the character of party rivalry become ever more bland and vapid. One cannot call this kind of politics non- or anti-democratic, because so much of it results from politicians' anxieties about their relations with citizens. At the same time it is difficult to dignify it as democracy itself, because so many citizens have been reduced to the role of manipulated, passive, rare participants.

It is in this context that we can understand remarks made by certain leading British New Labour figures concerning the need to develop institutions of democracy going beyond the idea of elected representatives in a parliament, and citing the use of focus groups as an example (Mulgan 1997). The idea is preposterous. A focus group is entirely in the control of its organizers; they select the participants, the issues and the way in which they are to be discussed and the outcome analysed. However, politicians in a period of post-democracy confront a public that is confused and passive in developing its own agenda. It is certainly under-standable that they should see a focus group as a more scientific guide to popular opinion than the crude and inadequate devices of their mass party claiming to be the voice of the people, which is the alternative historically offered by the labour movement's model of democracy.

Virtually all the formal components of democracy survive within post-democracy, which is compatible with the complexity of a 'post-' period. However, we should expect to see some erosion in the longer term, as we move, blasé and disillusioned, further and further away from maximal democracy. The largely quiescent response of US public opinion to the scandal of the 2000 presidential election was evidence that this had happened. In Britain there are signs of weariness with democracy in both Con-servative and New Labour approaches to local govern-ment, the functions of which are gradually disappearing, with little opposition, into either central government agencies or private firms. We should also expect the removal of some fundamental supports of democracy and therefore a parabolic return to some elements characteris-tic of pre-democracy. The globalization of business inter-ests and fragmentation of the rest of the population does this, shifting political advantage away from those seeking to reduce inequalities of wealth and power in favour of those wishing to return them to levels of the pre-democratic past.

Some of the substantive consequences of this can already be seen in many countries. The welfare state gradually becomes residualized as something for the deserving poor rather than a range of universal rights of citizenship; trade unions exist on the margins of society; the role of the state as policeman and incarcerator returns to prominence; the wealth gap between rich and poor grows; taxation becomes less redistributive; politicians respond primarily to the concerns of a handful of business leaders whose special interests are allowed to be translated into public policy; the poor gradually cease to take any interest in the process whatsoever and do not even vote, returning voluntarily to the position they were forced to occupy in pre-democracy. That the USA, the world's most future-oriented society and in the past a pioneer of democratic advance, should also be the one to show the strongest such return to an earlier time is only explicable in terms of the parabola of democracy.

There is profound ambiguity in the post-democratic tendency towards growing suspicion of politics and the desire to submit it to close regulation, again seen most prominently in the USA. An important element of the democratic moment was the popular demand that the power of government should be used to challenge concentrations of private power. An atmosphere of cynicism about politics and politicians, low expectations of their achievements, and close control of their scope and power therefore suits the agenda of those wishing to rein back the active state, as in the form of the welfare state and Keynesian state, precisely in order to liberate and deregulate that private power. At least in western societies, unregulated private power was as much a feature of pre-democratic societies as unregulated state power.

Post-democracy also makes a distinctive contribution to the character of political communication. If one looks back at the different forms of political discussion of the inter- and post-war decades one is surprised at the relative similarity of language and style in government documents, serious journalism, popular journalism, party manifestos and politicians' public speeches. There were certainly differences of vocabulary and complexity between a serious official report designed for the policy-making community and a mass-circulation newspaper, but compared with today the gap was small. Today the language of documents discussed among policy-makers themselves remains more or less similar to what it was then. But mass-circulation newspaper discussion, government material aimed at the mass public, and party manifestos are totally different. They rarely aspire to any complexity of language or argument. Someone accustomed to such a style suddenly requiring to access a document of serious debate would be at a loss as to how to understand it. Television news presentations, hovering uneasily between the two worlds, probably thereby provide a major service in helping people make such links.

We have become accustomed to hear politicians not speaking like normal people, but presenting glib and finely honed statements which have a character all of their own. We call these 'sound bites', and, having dismissively labelled them, think no more about what is going on. Like the language of tabloid newspapers and party literature, this form of communication resembles neither the ordinary speech of the person in the street, nor the language of true political discussion. It is designed to be beyond the reach of scrutiny by either of these two main modes of democratic discourse.

This raises several questions. The mid-century population was on average less well educated than today's. Were they able to understand the political discussions presented to them? They certainly turned out for elections more consistently than their successors; and in many countries they regularly bought newspapers that addressed them at that higher level, paying for them a higher proportion of their incomes than we do today.

To understand what has happened since the middle of the last century, we need to look at a slightly broader historical picture. Taken by surprise, first by the demand for, then by the reality of, democracy, politicians struggled for the first part of the century to find means of addressing the new mass public. For a period it seemed that only manipulative demagogues like Hitler, Mussolini and Stalin had discovered the secret of power through mass communication. Democratic politicians were placed on roughly equal discursive terms with their electorates through the clumsiness of their attempts at mass speech. Then the US advertising industry began to develop its skills, with a particular boost coming from the development of commercial television. The persuasion business was born as a profession. By far the dominant part of this remained devoted to the art of selling goods and services, but politics and other users of persuasion tagged along eagerly behind, extrapolating from the innovations of the advertising industry and making themselves as analogous as possible to the business of selling products so that they could reap maximum advantage from the new techniques.

We have now become so accustomed to this that we take it for granted that a party's programme is a 'product', and that politicians try to 'market' us their message. But it is not really at all obvious. Other successful models of how to talk to large numbers of people were potentially available among religious preachers, schoolteachers and serious popular journalists. A particularly striking example of the last was the British writer George Orwell, who strove to make mass political communication both an art form and something deeply serious. (See Crick 1980 for a particularly fine account of this.) From the 1930s to the 1950s there was considerable emulation of the Orwellian approach in British popular journalism. But little of it survives today. Popular journalism, like politics, began to model itself on advertising copy: very brief messages requiring extremely low concentration spans; the use of words to form high-impact images instead of arguments appealing to the intellect. Advertising is not a form of rational dialogue. It does not build up a case based on evidence, but associates its products with a particular imagery. You cannot answer it back. Its aim is not to engage in discussion but to persuade to buy. Adoption of its methods has helped politicians to cope with the problem of communicating to a mass public; but it has not served the cause of democracy itself.

A further form taken by the degradation of mass political communication is the growing personalization of electoral politics. Totally personality-based election campaigning used to be characteristic of dictatorships and of electoral politics in societies with weakly developed systems of parties and debate. With occasional exceptions (like Konrad Adenauer and Charles de Gaulle) it was much less prominent during the democratic moment; its insistent return now is another aspect of the parabola. Promotion of the claimed charismatic qualities of a party leader, and pictures and film footage of his or her person striking appropriate poses, increasingly take the place of debate over issues and conflicting interests. Italian politics was long free of this, until in the 2001 general election Silvio Berlusconi organized the entire centre-right campaign around his own persona, using omnipresent and carefully rejuvenated pictures of himself, a strong contrast with the far more party-oriented style that Italian politics had adopted after the fall of Mussolini. Instead of using this as the basis of attack, the immediate and sole response of the centre-left was to identify a sufficiently photogenic individual within its own leadership in order to try to copy as much as possible the Berlusconi campaign.

More extreme still was the role of personality campaigning in the exceptional Californian gubernatorial election of 2003, when the film actor Arnold Schwarzenegger waged a successful campaign with no policy content that was based almost entirely on the fact that he was a well-known Hollywood star. In the first Dutch general election of 2002, Pim Fortuyn not only based a new party entirely around his own person, but named the party after himself (Lijst Pim Fortuyn), with such dramatic success that it continued despite (or because of) his own assassination shortly before the election. The party then collapsed through internal feuding soon afterwards. The Fortuyn phenomenon is both an example of post-democracy and a kind of attempted response to it. It used a charismatic personality to articulate a vague and incoherent set of policies, which reflected no clearly articulated interests except unease about numbers of recent immigrants into the Netherlands. It appealed to sections of a population that have lost their former sense of political identity, though it does not help them find a new one. Dutch society is a particularly acute case of rapid loss of political identity. Not only has it, like most other Western European societies, experienced a loss of clear class identities, it has also experienced a rapid loss in salience of the religious identities that were until the 1970s fundamentally important in enabling Dutch people to find their specific cultural as well as political identities within their wider society.

However, although some of those who have tried to articulate a 'new', post-identity approach to politics, such as Tony Blair or Silvio Berlusconi, celebrate the decline of such kinds of identity, Fortuyn's movement also expressed dissatisfaction with that very state of affairs. Much of his campaigning lamented the lack of 'clarity' in the political positions adopted by most other Dutch politicians, who he claimed (with considerable accuracy) tried to solve problems of declining clarity in the profile of the electorate itself by appealing to a vague middle mass. In finding an appeal to identity based on hostility to immigrants, Fortuyn was not so unusual; this has become a feature of contemporary politics almost everywhere – an issue to which we shall return.

In addition to being an aspect of the decline from serious discussion, the recourse to show business for ideas of how to attract interest in politics, the growing incapacity of modern citizens to work out what their interests are, and the increasing technical complexity of issues, the personality phenomenon can be explained as a response to some of the problems of post-democracy itself. Although no-one involved in politics has any intention of abandoning the advertising industry model of communication, identification of specific cases of it, in current British jargon stigmatized as 'spin', is tantamount to an accusation of dishonesty. Politicians have thereby acquired a reputation for deep untrustworthiness as a personality characteristic. The increasing exposure of their private lives to media gaze, as blaming, complaining and investigating replace constructive citizenship, has the same consequence. Electoral competition then takes the form of a search for individuals of character and integrity. The search is futile because a mass election does not provide data on which to base such assessments. Instead what occurs is that politicians promote images of their personal wholesomeness and integrity, while their opponents only intensify the search through the records of their private lives to find evidence of the opposite.

Exploring post-democracy

In the chapters that follow I shall explore both the causes and the political consequences of the slide towards post-democratic politics. The causes are complex. Entropy of maximal democracy has to be expected, but the question then arises of what emerges to fill the political vacuum that this creates. Today the most obvious force doing this has been economic globalization. Large corporations have frequently outgrown the governance capacity of individual nation states. If they do not like the regulatory or fiscal regime in one country, they threaten to move to another, and increasingly states compete in their willingness to offer them favourable conditions, as they need the investment. Democracy has simply not kept pace with capitalism's rush to the global. The best it can manage are certain international groupings of states, but even the most important by far of these, the European Union, is a clumsy pygmy in relation to the agile corporate giants. And anyway its democratic quality, even by minimal standards, is weak. I shall take up some of these themes in chapter 2, where we shall consider the limitations of globalization as well as the importance of a separate but related phenomenon: the rise of the firm as an institution, its implications for the typical mechanisms of democratic government, and therefore its role in bending the parabola.

Alongside the strengthening of the global firm and firms in general has been a weakening of the political importance of ordinary working people. This partly reflects occupational changes that will be discussed in chapter 3. The decline of those occupations that generated the labour organizations that powered the rise of popular political demands has left us with a fragmented, politically passive population that has not generated organizations to articulate its demands. More than that, the decline of Keynesianism and of mass production has reduced the economic importance of the mass of the population: the parabola of working-class politics.

These changes in the political place of major social groupings have important consequences for the relationship between political parties and the electorate. This is particularly relevant to parties of the left, which historically have represented the groups now being pushed back to the margins of political importance; but since many of the problems concern the mass electorate in general the issue extends much wider. The model of parties developed for coping with the rise of democracy has gradually and subtly been transformed into something else, that of the post-democratic party. This is the subject of chapter 4.

Many readers might object that, especially by the time we have reached the discussion in chapter 4, I am myself concerned only with a self-referential political world. Does it matter to ordinary citizens what kinds of person walks the corridors of political influence? Is it not just all a courtly game with no real social consequences? One can refute that contention by looking at many policy areas, demonstrating to what extent the growing dominance of business lobbies over most other interests has distorted the real policy delivery side of government activity, with real consequences for citizens. There is here space to select just one example. In chapter 5 I consider the impact of post-democratic politics on the currently important theme of organizational reform of public services. Finally, in chapter 6, I ask if there is anything that we can do about the disturbing tendencies that have been described.

2

The Global Firm: The Key Institution of the Post-Democratic World

For most of the twentieth century the European left completely failed to appreciate the significance of the firm as an institution. Initially it seemed to be solely a device for reaping profits for owners and exploiting workers. The advantages of market sensitivity to consumers' demands that the firm embodied were largely lost on the generally poor working class, who had only limited chances to express consumer preferences. Then, in the easy years of growing affluence of the third quarter of the twentieth century, when mass consumerism began to take hold, the firm could be taken for granted as a convenient milch-cow.

During this Keynesian period virtually all parties emphasized macro-economic policy. Individual companies were assumed to have no difficulty exploring and exploiting niches in product markets that were kept buoyant by the macro-policies. Those of the neo-liberal right who stressed the primacy of micro-economics and the problems of the firm were largely disregarded. In some ways this suited firms themselves: in setting a context of economic stability and not becoming involved in the fine details of what firms did, governments did not intervene much in their affairs.

The collapse of the Keynesian paradigm amid the inflationary crises of the 1970s changed all this. As aggregate demand levels were no longer guaranteed, product markets became unreliable. This was intensified by other developments: rapid technological change and innovation; intensifying global competition; and more demanding consumers. Companies that had jogged along unenterprisingly found the ground cut from their feet. Differences between the successful and the unsuccessful became exaggerated; bankruptcies and unemployment grew. The survival of only reasonably successful firms could no longer be taken for granted. Lobbies and pressure groups working for the interests of the corporate sector were more likely to be listened to, just as complaints about a draught from an invalid have to be taken more seriously than those from a healthy person.

A number of other changes followed which, while they made the firm into a robust and demanding creature, anything but an invalid, continued, paradoxically, to have the same consequence of enforcing increased attention to its demands. It is becoming a cliché of political debate that globalization has been fundamental to this. It obviously intensifies competition, and this exposes the vulnerabilities of individual firms. But the survivors of this competition are those who become tough, and the toughness is expressed not just or even primarily against competitors, but against governments and workforces. If the owners of a global firm do not find a local fiscal or labour regime congenial, they will threaten to go elsewhere. They can therefore have access to governments, and influence the policies being pursued by them, far more effectively than can its nominal citizens, even if they do not live there, have formal citizen rights there, or pay taxes. In *The Work of Nations* (1991) Robert Reich wrote about both this group and the highly paid professionals whose skills are demanded across the world, and the problems posed by the fact that they have considerable power but owe loyalty to no particular human community. Similar options are not available to the mass of the population, who remain more or less rooted to their native nation state, whose laws they must obey and taxes they must pay.

In many respects this resembles the situation in pre-Revolutionary France, where the monarchy and aristocracy were exempt from taxation but monopolized political power, while the middle classes and peasantry paid taxes but had no political rights. The manifest injustice of this provided much of the energy and ferment behind the initial struggle for democracy. Members of the global corporate elite do nothing so blatant as taking away our right to vote. (We are in the parabola of democracy, not coming full circle.) They merely point out to a government that, if it persists in maintaining, say, extensive labour rights, they will not invest in the country. All major parties in that country, fearing to call their bluff, tell their electorates that outmoded labour regulation must be reformed. The electorate then, whether conscious of the deregulation proposal or not, duly votes for those parties, there being few others to choose from. Deregulation of the labour market can therefore be said to have been freely chosen by the democratic process.

Similarly, firms might insist on reduced corporate taxation if they are to continue to invest in a country. As governments oblige them, the fiscal burden shifts from firms to individual taxpayers, who in turn become resentful of high tax levels. The major parties respond to this by conducting general elections as tax-cutting auctions; the electorate duly favours the party offering the biggest tax cuts, and a few years later discovers that its public services have severely deteriorated. But they had voted for it; the policy had democratic legitimacy (Przeworski and Mese-guer Yebra 2002).

We must be careful not to exaggerate all this. The image of totally footloose capital is a curiously shared distortion of the left and the right. The former use it to present a picture of business interests totally out of control. The latter use it to argue against all measures of labour regula-tion and taxation that corporations find irksome. In reality, not only are many firms far from global, but even trans-national giants are constrained by their existing patterns of investment, expertise and networks from skipping around the world in search of the lowest taxes and worst labour conditions. They have what economists call 'sunk costs', which means that moving is costly. There was a sharp reminder of this during 2000, when both BMW and Ford decided to reduce their operations in Britain in favour of their German plants. Although an important part of the argument concerned the excessive strength of sterling, another was that it was more difficult and costly to close down an operation in Germany. In other words, the very efforts which Conservative and New Labour govern-ments had made to attract inward investment by stressing how flexible British regulations were made it more likely that inward investing firms would close a British factory. Easy come meant easy go.

However, while an economy like the German one might be more likely than the British to retain its existing manufacturing activities, the British stance might be more likely to attract more new firms, provided it continues to offer footloose global firms what they say they want. If this policy is successful, gradually all countries will start to imitate it, competing with each other to offer inward investors everything they ask for, leading to the predicted 'race to the bottom' in labour standards, tax-ation levels and hence quality of public services (apart from those like roads and labour skills directly wanted by the inward investors). So far this race has been slow to develop, largely because pro-labour and pro-welfare interests in some (though by no means all) European Union countries have retained more power than in the UK (Kiser and Laing 2001). Gradually, however, this could well erode. Whatever aspirations might emerge from the democratic processes of politics, a population needing employment has to bend the knee to global companies' demands.

Exaggerated or not, globalization clearly contributes to the constraints imposed on democracy, which is a system that has difficulty rising above national levels. But the implications of the rising importance of the firm as an institution, which is one aspect of the globalization question, go considerably further and have negative implications for democracy of a subtler kind.

The phantom firm

During the 1980s many large corporations tried to develop a company culture, or 'whole company' approach. This meant shaping everything about them for targeted pursuit of competitive success. In particular, the personalities of their employees and the quality of their loyalty to the organization were to be fashioned according to a central plan. This was the period when Japan was seen as the prime model of economic success, and large Japanese corporations had pursued such strategies particularly effectively. For many firms this became an argument why they should not allow external trade unions to represent their workers, or employers' associations to represent their own interests in collective bargaining, or even trade associations their more technical and marketing interests. They had to be free to act and lobby for themselves.

This helped set the stage of the new prominence of the individual firm rather than the business association, but its subsequent development took a curious political path. Enthusiasm for corporate cultures has been countered by two new master tendencies, which have followed the replacement of the Japanese by the US corporate model as the one which everyone is seeking to imitate: (i) the tendency for firms to change their identity very rapidly as they engage in take-overs, mergers and frequent reorganizations, and try to escape any bad reputations they have acquired in the past; (ii) the growing casualization of the workforce (including such developments as temporary labour contracts, franchising and the imposition of self-employed status on people who are *de facto* employees).

These changes are a response to what has become the overwhelming demand of firms: flexibility. This has been made their central operational priority by a combination of the uncertainty of today's markets and the new centrality of stock exchanges following global financial deregulation. Maximizing shareholder value has become the overriding objective, and this requires a capacity to switch activities rapidly. Strong business lobbies in continental Europe and Japan urge adoption of this essentially Anglo-American system of corporate governance. There has been a heavy ideological component in this campaign. In practice, the great majority of firms' investment funds continue to come from retained earnings rather than from the stock market. This occurs in continental European economies, where retained earnings are complemented by bank loans rather than equity finance, but it is more important in the Anglophone economies, heartland of the stock-exchange-driven economy, where equity finance accounts for only a small proportion of investment funds (Corbett and Jenkinson 1996).

Having full flexibility of this kind goes beyond the now familiar process of retaining a core business but sub-contracting ancillary activities. *Having a core business itself becomes a rigidity.* The most advanced firms out-source and sub-contract more or less everything except a strategic headquarters financial decision-making capacity, which manages the brand, but has very little to do with actual production. Information technology is of great assistance to them in the complex organization tasks that this involves. The Internet can be used both to assemble orders from customers and to commission production and distribution from a disaggregated set of production units, which can be rapidly changed to adjust to shifting circumstances. The object of a successful firm is to locate itself primarily in the financial sector, because this is where capital is at its most mobile, and to sub-contract everything else it does to small, insecure units. Then, as Naomi Klein analysed so skilfully in her book *No Logo* (2000), if all the work of making a product can be contracted out, the firm itself can concentrate on the sole task of developing brand images. The role of the successful firm, liberated from any substantive tasks, is just to associate brand names with attractive images, concepts, celebrity figures; products bearing the brand will be bought because of these associations, almost irrespective of their actual quality.

The bewildering pace of mergers, and the phantom character of firms which constitute temporary, anonymous financial accumulations for the electronic co-ordination of a mass of disaggregated activities, lead many commentators to see here the final dissolution of capital as a socio-political category, a major stage in the end of the class divisions of old industrial society (e.g. Castells 1996; Giddens 1998). The early twenty-first-century firm can thus seem a weaker institution than its predecessors: no longer the solid organization with a large headquarters building and strong presence, but a soft, flexible, constantly changing will of the wisp.

Nothing could be further from the truth. Its capacity to deconstruct itself is the most extreme form taken by the firm in its dominance of contemporary society. The classic firm had more or less stable ownership concentrations, a workforce of direct employees, whom it often encouraged to achieve long service, and a reputation with customers, which it acquired over a prolonged period. The archetypal contemporary firm is owned by a constantly changing constellation of asset holders, who trade their shares in it electronically. It makes use of a diversity of labour-service contract forms in order to bring together fluctuating combinations of workers and dispense with the need to have any actual employees. Those who work for it are rarely in a position to identify and target it. Rather than seeking a reputation for quality for its products, it frequently changes its name and range of activities, using advertising and marketing techniques to acquire temporary images, which can in turn be replaced and re-engineered after a relatively short period. Customers have difficulty in establishing its track record. Invisibility becomes a weapon.

Behind the fluctuations two constants remain. First, the identity of the major real owners of corporate wealth changes far more slowly: it is the same groups, more or less the same individuals, who keep appearing in new shapes and guises. The two economies which demonstrate the new form of flexible capitalism in the most advanced degree, the UK and the USA, are also the two advanced societies which are experiencing increasing inequality in property ownership, despite far wider nominal share ownership than in the past. Individual bundles of capital might deconstruct themselves, but not the ultimate owners. Second, however much individual firms may change their identity, the general concept of the firm as an institution acquires – partly as a result of this flexibility itself – greater prominence within society. This requires closer scrutiny, as it raises some major issues of post-democracy.

The firm as an institutional model

In many ways the flexible phantom firm is highly responsive to customers' wants. If one firm finds that it can maximize its profits by moving out of the construction of steel products and into the manufacture of mobile phones, another is likely to take its place in the former activity. This is the creative turmoil of the market. However, not all wants are best served by such a model. There may be strong reasons for ensuring that everyone should have access to certain goods and services, which it will be unprofitable for firms within a free market to produce. This is a familiar problem, to which the normal answer is that this indicates the role of government. But to acknowledge this requires acceptance that the *modus operandi* of government and private firm differ in certain respects. To take just one simple example: supermarkets place themselves on major out-of-town traffic routes where the majority of profitable customers can gain access to them. This leaves a residuum of people who find it very difficult to go shopping, but these are poor people whose small purchases it is not worth the supermarkets' while to bother about. This is sometimes considered a minor scandal, but this is small compared with what would happen in the following case. Imagine that a public authority responsible for providing schools in a town announces that, as part of its policy of market testing and best-value procedures, it has been taking lessons in cost-effective location from consultants to supermarket chains. Henceforth it will be closing most

of its schools and will reopen a small number of very large
ones, located on motorway access points. Research
has shown it that the small numbers of pupils whose
parents do not have cars are likely to be poor educational
performers. Therefore, in addition to considerable cost
savings resulting from the closure of many schools, the
town's scores in school league tables will improve as a
result of the inability of these poorly performing children
to attend school.

Everyone can think of many reasons why this is
unacceptable and never practised. In doing so one makes
use of concepts like the need for universal access to essential public services, which mark out the essential differences between public-service and commercial provision.
Government is, however, increasingly incapable of spelling
out where the boundaries of these two lie. At moments of
need, appeal will be made back to ideas of public service
and citizen entitlement, forged some time between the late
nineteenth and mid-twentieth centuries. But the relationship of these ideas, held in static veneration as museum
pieces, and the bustling forces of commercialization,
which are the focus of virtually all new thinking and policy
initiatives for service delivery within government, is rarely
formulated coherently or even examined. There is real
conflict here, and it is being glossed over, because governments envy the phantom firm its flexibility and apparent
efficiency, and try to imitate it almost heedlessly. As we
shall see in chapter 5, government increasingly renounces
any distinctive role for public service (which stresses a duty
to provide citizens with more or less equal services to a
high standard), and requires its departments to act as firms
(which stresses a duty of providing a service to that quality
which is required by the meeting of financial targets). To
achieve this change, parts of the public service are either
privatized or contracted out to firms, or, staying within the

public sector, are required to act as though they were firms. Like the phantom firm, government is trying gradually to divest itself of all direct responsibilities for the conduct of public services. In this way it hopes to avoid dependence on the vagaries of real reputation. But in doing so it relinquishes its claim to the special functions that can be performed only by the public service. This further leads to the conclusion that persons from the private corporate sector should manage public services, as it is only their expertise that is relevant now.

Undermining government self-confidence

As we shall see in more detail in chapter 5, one major consequence of all this is an extreme lack of confidence on the part of the public services that they can do anything well unless they are under the guidance of the corporate sector. Eventually this becomes self-justifying. As more and more state functions are sub-contracted to the private sector, so the state begins to lose competence to do things which once it managed very well. Gradually it even loses touch with the knowledge necessary to understand certain activities. It is therefore forced to sub-contract further and buy consultancy services to tell it how to do its own job. Government becomes a kind of institutional idiot, its every ill-informed move being anticipated in advance and therefore discounted by smart market actors. From this follows the core policy recommendation of contemporary economic orthodoxy: the state had best do nothing at all, beyond guaranteeing the freedom of the markets.

As government increasingly divests itself of autonomous competences, it concedes to neo-liberal ideology what had once been a powerful argument in favour of active government: the capacity of the actor at the centre to perceive what cannot be seen by individual firms. This had been a central rationale for Keynesian policies in the first place. The experience of the 1920s and 1930s showed that the market might by itself be unable to stimulate a recovery, but that the state might be able to do so. Today's assumptions about the poverty of the state's knowledge and its likely incompetence rule this out. Meanwhile, as knowledge relevant to governance and regulation is seen as residing almost uniquely in profit-seeking private corporations, these are encouraged to deploy that knowledge in a way that enhances their own profits.

This can be distorting and, eventually, simply corrupt. The accounting scandals affecting a number of the world's leading corporations since 2002 are a major instance of this. The task of regulating corporate accounts has long been delegated to a class of auditing firms, but during the 1990s two developments turned this practice into a major source of dishonesty and fraud. First, no political or legal objections were raised to the growing practice of accountancy firms selling other management services to the firms whose accounts they were checking: the regulated became the customers of the regulators, and so the regulators were careful not to displease the regulated. Second, the share-market boom of the 1990s depended heavily on future expectations rather than achieved performance. If the presentation of a firm's accounts suggested that it was likely to do well in the future, its shares would rise, irrespective of its current performance in product markets. It was the accountancy firms who were trusted to pronounce on firms' future prospects. Only in a climate where it had become axiomatic that private firms would perform effectively in essentially public regulatory capacities could it have been possible for such a folly to have been allowed to proceed until it caused major damage.

Meanwhile, the despised institution of government is tending to resolve itself into three parts: a number of activities which it tries increasingly to convert into market form; a dreary, residual, burdensome set of obligations which the private sector will not take off its hands; and an image-creating, purely political component. It is not surprising that government is coming to be seen as a mixture of incompetence to provide real services plus parasitic spinning and electioneering. Only France, where left and right alike share the republican tradition of the state as a major formative force creating civil society, more or less resists the trend – though that tradition seems powerless to prevent practices whereby public-service contracts and privatized services are awarded to politically favoured firms and the business friends of politicians.

The corporate elite and political power

Firms are not simply organizations, but concentrations of power. Their pattern of ownership produces concentrations of private wealth, and the more important firms become, the more important becomes the class of capital owners. Further, the great majority of firms are organized in a manner that gives considerable authority to their senior managers. This becomes increasingly the case as the Anglo-American model of the firm, concentrating all power on a chief executive responsible solely to shareholders, pushes out various other forms of capitalism which recognize a wider range of stakeholders. The more powerful the firm becomes as an organizational form, the more powerful become the individuals who occupy these positions. They become even more powerful as government concedes to them the organization of its own activities and bows to the superiority of their expertise. In addition to dominating the economy itself, they become the class that also dominates the running of government.

There is yet another consequence. As government withdraws from the extensive funding role it acquired in the Keynesian and social democratic period, so organizations operating in non-profit areas turn elsewhere for financial sponsorship. As wealth and power gravitate towards the corporate sector, this becomes the main potential source of such sponsorship. This brings persons from the business sector into powerful positions as they decide what they might sponsor. In the UK this has now reached the point where think tanks associated with the Labour Party have to find firms willing to fund individual items of their policy research, which often means that firms are sponsoring policy work on topics where they have a direct interest in the outcome. Even some UK government advisory bodies depend on company donations to fund part of their work.

The reason why some of these activities were not in the corporate sector in the first place was often precisely that it was considered inappropriate. For example, there are clear problems if pharmaceutical firms become the main sponsors of medical research – but that is exactly what is happening as governments encourage universities to rely increasingly on sponsorship rather than public funding. In the past, corporations usually channelled their support for scientific and cultural activity through trusts managed quite autonomously from the firms themselves. This was during the period of democratic sensitivities, when people would look askance at direct involvement in what were seen as non-commercial activities by centres of commercial power and interest. Today sponsorship is less often mediated in this way, and firms are likely to fund activities directly.

In order to encourage scientific, cultural and other non-commercial activities to seek private sponsorship, governments increasingly make their own financing of such activities dependent on success in attracting such sponsorship: a local theatre or a university department will get public help if it can first make itself attractive to private donors. This further strengthens the power of wealthy people, enabling them to determine the allocation of public funds, as public money follows the allocative decisions made by the private sponsor. A similar example is the practice, originating in the USA but rapidly spreading, of permitting charitable donations to be offset against liability for taxation. The objective in doing this is to reduce the funding that government itself must undertake. Its consequence, however, is that wealthy corporations and individuals have been able not only to decide which of a number of activities to favour with their own money, but simultaneously to pre-empt the pattern of public spending, which often originally existed precisely in order to assert priorities different from those which would be chosen by the rich.

A further consequence still of these developments is that entrepreneurs and company managers acquire very privileged access to politicians and civil servants. Since their success and expertise depend entirely on their ability to maximize value for their firms' shareholders, they must be expected to use that access for the benefit of those individual firms. This becomes particularly the case if relations between government and an economic sector flow not through associations representing firms in the sector, but through individual large corporations. This is starting to predominate even in Germany and Sweden, two countries where for so long firms worked through powerful and highly effective collective organizations. In the late 1990s the social-democrat-led German government engaged employees of leading private firms to devise its corporate tax policies; not surprisingly, the result was a major shift in the German tax burden away from large corporations towards small firms and workers.

Further, as government out-sources and sub-contracts ever more of its activities – usually doing so on the advice of persons from the corporate sector – so the potential value of such access in winning government contracts increases. If, as argued in the previous chapter, one characteristic of current politics is a shift to the liberal model of lobbying and cause presentation as opposed to the politics of parties, this is a serious development. It suggests that the politics of the lobby will be shifting ever further towards the enhancement of the power of major corporations and those who hold key offices within them. The power that they already possess within their firms becomes translated into a far more extensive political power. This challenges severely the democratic balance.

The special place of media corporations

The power of a politically highly relevant group of corporations – those in the media industry – is in fact involved directly in reductions of choice and the debasement of political language and communication which are important components of the poor health of democracy. This is the case in two separate ways. First, the press and, increasingly, radio and television are part of the commercial sector of society – rather than, say, the charitable or education sectors, as they might well have been. This means that news broadcasts and all other politically relevant communications need to be modelled on a certain form of the idea of a marketable product. The attention of the reader, listener or viewer has to be grabbed quickly if one media firm is to take custom from another. This prioritizes extreme simplification and sensationalization, which in turn degrade the quality of political discussion and reduce the competence of citizens. Oversimplification and sensationalization are not built into the market and commercialization as such: markets for rare books, high-performance cars and fine wines – among many others – respect the purchaser's needs for carefully considered judgement and the provision of rich information. Such markets are even found to a limited extent within the mass media, in newspapers and programmes designed for highly educated people, who can access complex argument without much mental effort. It is the particular character of the mass market for news, and the transitory nature of the product, that make it unsuitable for seriousness. Political actors themselves are then forced into the same mode if they are to retain some control over how they formulate their own utterances: if they do not adopt the style of rapid, eye-catching banality, journalists will completely rewrite the message. The headline was the father of the sound bite.

One can perform a little thought experiment to see how this operates. Imagine that schools approached the task of communication as newspapers do, and vice versa. Every day teachers would run the risk that, if they did not rapidly catch the attention of their pupils, the following morning the pupils would take themselves off to a different school. It is doubtful if algebra, the structure of carbon atoms or French irregular verbs would ever be taught to any child. In fact, something of this nightmare has occurred: teachers have to compete for the attention of children who spend many of their leisure hours watching television. It is remarkable that this possibility is almost never raised in expressions of public concern over educational standards. Could this possibly be related to the fact that such expressions of concern are mainly managed by mass media owners?

Now, it could be objected here that, sooner or later, parents and pupils would realize that an education made up of eye-catching and easily digested, exciting snippets of knowledge led nowhere, and in particular did not equip pupils for good positions in the labour market. The market for knowledge would thus correct itself, and good schools would be rewarded by increased participation. But in the case of mass political communication, there is no source of such correction. The analogy to the test of pupils discovering that their superficial education would be no use would be people discovering that their newspapers and television programmes had not equipped them to be effective political citizens. But that test never comes, certainly not in a perceptible form. People may feel vaguely aware that they have little understanding of what is going on in government and politics, and they may feel bewildered that all they hear about are political personalities, scandals and inflated bits of trivia. But the trail back from there to the logic of a certain kind of fast-moving market is impossible for them to find.

To find the vice versa analogy, the media operating more like a school, one does not need so much imagination. This was the original model of the British Broadcasting Corporation, and some other public service broadcasters around the democratic world. These broadcasters had the mission, explicit in the BBC's case, to 'inform, educate and entertain'. Remnants of this model survive in the BBC and, to a lesser extent, in the regulated part of private-sector television. Forms of public regulation – at long arm's length from political interference – provided both a form of protection from immediate market pressure and an obligation to respect goals other than those of grabbing rapid attention. This model has been in decline for some time. Obligations on public-service programme makers to watch their viewer ratings in relation to those of their private-sector rivals necessarily draw them precisely into attention-grabbing. This process has intensified as technological developments have removed the earlier limitation imposed on numbers of broadcast sources by the original system of air waves, creating opportunities for satellite, cable and digital services. Also, print journalism and the broadcast media tend to take each other as the source of stories. This becomes one-sided: it brings the priorities of print journalism and private broadcasting into public-service broadcasting, while the requirement of rapid attention-grabbing prevents the former from picking up much from the latter which does not already take this form.

The commercial model is therefore triumphing over other concepts of mass political communication. Politics and other types of news have been increasingly redefined as items of very short-term consumer spending. The consumer has triumphed over the citizen (see Davies and Graham 1997 for a fine account of this process).

The second reason for concern over the role played by press, radio and television in mediating political communication is that control over these media is concentrated in a very small number of hands. Ironically, the growth of new technologies for carrying information has not led to increased diversity in providers, unless one takes account of very small minority-interest channels. The problem is that the technologies needed for true mass circulation are extremely expensive, and only vast corporations are in a position to acquire them. In the UK – admittedly an extreme case – one firm (News Corporation) is a satellite television monopolist (BSkyB), owns newspapers as diverse as *The Times* and *The Sun*, and has interlocking relations with other media providers. And News Corporation is an international enterprise, the British interests of which are only a part. In Italy, the prime minister is the main figure by far in the private media sector (as well as exercising increasing influence over public broadcasting).

Even where there is competition, this is unlikely to bring diversity given the economic circumstances of mass media markets. When producers identify a large, rather homogeneous mass market of consumers, they all try to target their activities on it, which means that they all try to offer more or less the same. Diversity will appear under only two circumstances. First, there can be forms of media provision, as was formally the case of many public-service broadcasters, whose mission is different from that of maximizing a single audience. Second, commercial producers will produce diversity if they can easily identify a segmented market rather than a predominant mass; they then choose to target their activities on particular segments. This happens in the case of the 'quality' press, which targets itself on the small but generally prosperous segment of well-educated readers.

Control over politically relevant news and information, a resource vital to democratic citizenship, is coming under the control of a very small number of extremely wealthy individuals. And wealthy individuals, however much they might compete against each other, tend to share certain political perspectives, and have a very strong interest in using the resources at their command to fight for these. This does not just mean that some parties will be favoured rather than others by the media; the leaders of all parties are aware of this power and feel constrained by it when they formulate their programmes. Indeed, the kinds of concentration of ownership that have occurred could not have taken place had governments believed that they could dare to regulate in the interests of greater diversity and competition. Similar factors lie behind current pressures in most democracies for the role of public-service broadcasting to be pressed back to a small minority role, in favour of privately owned services.

Markets and classes

These developments in the growing political power of corporate interests are often presented in terms of the superior efficiency of markets. This is richly ironic, as the discussion of media corporations shows. A primary concern of the original eighteenth-century formulations of free-market economic doctrines by Adam Smith and others was to disentangle the political world and private entrepreneurs from each other, combating in particular the granting of monopolies and contracts to court favourites. As we shall see in chapter 5, much of the current activity of privatizing, contracting out and breaking down the separateness of public service and private firms returns us precisely to that dubious behaviour. We therefore witness another aspect of the parabola: a return to corporate political privilege under slogans of markets and free competition.

These things can only happen in societies which have lost the sense of a distinction between a public interest, guarded by public authorities careful to establish their own autonomous competence, and private interests looking after themselves. In pre-democratic times social elites which dominated economic and social life also monopolized political influence and positions in public life. The rise of democracy forced them at least to share space in the latter arenas with representatives of non-elite groups. Today, however, through the growing dependence of government on the knowledge and expertise of corporate executives and leading entrepreneurs, and the dependence of parties on their funds, we are steadily moving towards the establishment of a new dominant, combined political and economic, class. Not only do they have increasing power and wealth in their own right as societies become increasingly unequal, but they have also acquired the privileged political role that has always been the mark of true dominant classes. This is the central crisis of early twenty-first-century democracy.

There is a tendency in popular debate to see classes in terms of their cultural attributes – accent, dress, typical leisure pursuits – and therefore to declare the passing of class society if a particular set of these seems to decline. A far more serious meaning of the term identifies connections between different types of economic position and differential access to political power. This is far from declining. Its return is one of the most serious symptoms of the move to post-democracy, as the rise of the corporate elite parallels the decline in the vigour of creative democracy. It also establishes the link between the two problems established at the outset: the difficulties of egalitarian politics and the problems of democracy. One of the core political objectives of corporate elites is clearly to combat egalitarianism.

3

Social Class in Post-Democracy

The contemporary political orthodoxy that social class no longer exists is itself a symptom of post-democracy. In non-democratic societies, class privileges are proudly and arrogantly displayed, and subordinate classes are required to acknowledge their subordination; democracy challenges class privileges in the name of subordinate classes; post-democracy denies the existence of both privilege and subordination. While this denial can be vigorously contested through sociological analysis, it is certainly increasingly difficult for any other than increasingly confident shareholding and 'executive' classes to perceive themselves, or be perceived, as clearly defined social groups. This fact, and the imbalance produced, is a major cause of the problems of democracy.

The decline of the manual working class

By the end of the nineteenth century many skilled and some unskilled manual working groups had successfully organized themselves into trade unions in most parts of the now industrialized world and aspired to full political participation. There was considerable diversity in their

experience. In France, Switzerland and the USA the
achievement of formal male democracy predated the
growth of organized labour – with a paradoxical subsequent weakening of autonomously organized labour interests within those nation states. In some other cases – such
as Britain or Denmark – there was no once and for all
struggle for the suffrage, but a gradual growth. In many
other cases the struggle was difficult, violent, and in a
number of countries not achieved without shorter or
longer intervals of fascism or other forms of repression.
Despite this extreme diversity on the road to democracy,
almost all working classes experienced some degree of
political exclusion. There was also a strong sense of social
exclusion, most non-manual groups of the period
regarding even skilled manual workers as unfit to be suitable social companions. These factors were reinforced
by patterns of residential segregation that produced
single-class communities within neighbourhoods in most
industrial towns.

The divisions were never clear-cut, and other cleavages
often proved more important: except in Scandinavia,
differences between either Catholics and Protestants, or
the religious and secularists, or both, rivalled and often
overshadowed those between classes. However, there was
enough class-related political activity to make an impact.
The working class's relative social exclusion meant that its
discontent was constantly feared, and the poverty of parts
of it made it a worrying social problem – known in Catholic social debate as *la question sociale*. From the end of the
nineteenth century through to the third quarter of
the twentieth, finding ways of coping with the political
existence of this class was the major preoccupation of
domestic politics. While in strongly Catholic societies
the growth of autonomous workers' parties, and therefore
of open class-related political conflict, was weakened

by the strength of cross-class religious loyalty, the conflicts continued within Christian Democracy itself (Van
Kersbergen 1996).

For most of this time the class was growing in numbers,
and eventually also in income, so that it began to have an
effect on consumer markets as well as on policy for industrial relations and social welfare. It could plausibly be presented as the class of the future, and politicians of nearly all
parties knew that their own futures depended on their ability
to respond to its demands. Further, it was only when
economies were reshaped to make possible working-class
prosperity that the dynamism of mid-twentieth-century
mass-production capitalism took off.

Then, in the mid-1960s, the relative size of the manual
working class began to decline, first in North America, the
UK and Scandinavia, but gradually spreading to the rest of
the industrial world, including countries like Italy, France
and Spain which were still experiencing the decline of
agriculture associated with the rise of industrialism
(Crouch 1999a: ch. 4). Increased productivity and auto-
mation reduced the numbers of production workers
needed for a given unit of output, while employment in
administrative support activities, as well as in the various
services sectors (especially those associated with the welfare state), was growing steadily. The collapse of much
manufacturing in the 1980s and new waves of technological change in the 1990s eroded direct industrial
employment even further. While large numbers of people,
mainly men, continued to be manual workers, theirs was
was no longer the growing class of the future.

By the end of the twentieth century large parts of the
manual working class were engaged in defensive, protec-
tionist battles only. This was clearest and most dramatic in
the UK, where a formerly powerful labour movement
was brought down by a triple crisis: particularly rapid

deindustrialization resulting from the weakness of the country's industrial base; profound internecine conflict within the Labour Party; and a disastrously organized coal-mining strike. At the political level the Labour Party had been responding to the relative decline of the manual working class since at least the 1960s with some attempts to add various growing new non-manual groups to its coalition. This was particularly successful among men and women working in the public services, a major constituent of growth in non-manual employment at that time. The desperate leftward lurch of the party in the early 1980s, however, led it to forget its historical future-oriented role, and to attempt to forge coalitions of out-groups. In the deindustrializing north, in Liverpool, the party was forced back into a defiant proletarian redoubt – the same strategy that had been disastrously pursued by the French Communist Party for a longer period. In the new cosmopolitan, post-modern south, in London, there were attempts to forge a non-class rainbow coalition of the excluded, bringing together ethnic minorities and various identities primarily concerned with sexual orientation; a path also followed at that time by the US Democratic Party.

Both Liverpool and London strategies were destined to fail. The manual working class had begun the century as the future battering on the door, representing the collective interest in an age damaged by individualism: it brought the message of universal citizenship, and the possibilities of mass consumption in a society that knew only luxury goods for the rich and subsistence for the poor. By the end it represented history's losers: advocacy of the welfare state began to take the form of special appeals for compassion, not universal demands for citizenship. During the course of a century the class had described its parabola.

Elsewhere the pattern differed, sometimes considerably. Italy, Spain, Portugal and France were experiencing the shift to the left normally consequent on the decline of rural society, while their relatively strong communist parties were releasing themselves from Soviet dominance. Temporarily this led to the *increase* in labour movement strength referred to above. In Germany and Austria industrial employment remained strong for far longer, reducing the need for much adaptation of strategy, though by the 1990s this had the effect of leaving these countries' labour movements particularly resistant to change and adaptation. A declining industrial base did hit the Scandinavian movements and eroded their hegemonic position within their societies, but their strong role during the previous half-century prevented them from being marginalized. However, by the end of the twentieth century major and irreversible numerical decline had become the lot of manual working classes throughout the advanced world. The British experience of the 1980s remained an extreme case of political marginalization of the class, but not an exception.

The incoherence of other classes

It is more difficult to tell the class story of the rest – today the clear majority – of the population: the diverse and heterogeneous groups of professionals, administrators, clerical and sales workers, employees of financial institutions, of public bureaucracies and of welfare state organizations. Defined historically by education standards, incomes and working conditions superior to those of manual workers, most of these groups have often been reluctant to ally themselves to the interests and organizations of the working class. Most have, however, failed to generate much autonomous political profile at all.

Occupational organizations are usually weak (with very important exceptions among the professions and public service employees); voting behaviour is very mixed, lacking the clear biases of manual and true bourgeois classes.

This does not mean that people in these groups are apathetic about public life. On the contrary, as individuals they are the most likely to be found as active members of interest organizations and cause groups. But they are spread across a wide political spectrum of these, and therefore do not confront the political system with a clear agenda of demands – as does the resurgent capitalist class and once did the manual working class. They are often seen as politically closer to capital, in that in two-party systems they have tended historically to vote more for anti-socialist than for labour-based parties. But their position is more complex than that; they are, for example, strong supporters of the citizenship welfare state, especially services for health, education and pensions.

Closer inspection enables us to see more definite patterns within this middle mass. There is often a public/private division, the former far more likely to be unionized and – rather obviously – to be involved in organizations and lobbies for the protection of public services. The privatization of much of the public sector had an important electoral logic in the 1980s and 1990s, when centre-right parties in some countries were becoming opposed to public employees as a class and therefore seeking to reduce their numbers. (By the turn of the century, when left-of-centre parties started turning to the same policies, they encountered conflict with a core constituency.)

There are also major hierarchical divisions. Little or nothing connects routine office workers to senior managers, both the incomes and educational levels of the former often being lower than those of skilled manual workers. It is essential to recognize the role of gender here. In general, and of course with exceptions, the lower down a hierarchy, the lower the pay, and the lower the educational level, the more likely a non-manual worker is to be female. The gender divide provides at least as sharp a cultural cleavage within the non-manual hierarchy of the office or shop as the manual/non-manual one within the factory.

If one assumes that senior managerial and professional workers have good reasons to associate themselves with the political interests of capital – unless they work in the public services – the question why the lower ranks of the white-collar hierarchy have not developed a distinctive politics of their own becomes almost equivalent to the question: why did women not articulate an autonomous politics of the junior non-manual classes, in the way that men did for the skilled manual working class? This question is so important for the state of contemporary democracy that I will return to it in more detail below.

It will be objected to this account of the weakness of lower middle-class interests that, if anything, politicians are obsessed with this group and with responding to its concerns. However, these concerns are processed by the political system in a manner that defines them as entirely at one with those of business. This is what centre-right parties have been doing, with considerable success, for many years in order to ensure that these groups did not find a strong alliance with manual workers. If reformist groups like New Labour in Britain are at last successfully rivalling the centre-right in their appeal to them, it is because they have started doing the same, not because they are articulating wider concerns of these groups, which might be uncomfortable for the corporate elite. They are represented as having no discontents except with the quality of public services – which is increasingly taken to mean that they want these privatized. They are encouraged to seek no means of social improvement other than for themselves and their children obediently to climb the career ladders established by business elites. From this follows the obsessive concern of contemporary politics with education, as this seems to provide the main sure means of upward mobility. Since social mobility can only be enjoyed by a minority and in competition with everyone else, it is a very odd policy to offer as a general solution to life's discontents. This can temporarily be solved at a political, but not real, level by encouraging parents of the majority of pupils to blame schoolteachers for their children's relative lack of success.

The relationship to politics of the new social categories being created in the post-industrial economy therefore conforms closely to the post-democratic model: it is in relation to them that manipulative politics is most used; the group itself remains largely passive and lacks political autonomy. This is not surprising, as these are the groups that have grown in numbers during the post-democratic period. Intriguingly, they are not part of a parabola. Non-manual workers have not experienced a past period of political exclusion, as their numbers were very small in the pre-democratic period; during the high-tide of democracy they played a passive part as the busy forces of big business and organized (largely manual) labour struggled to find the social compromise. As a result they do not experience much of a change with post-democracy.

Women and democracy

There has, however, been one major recent point of change and disruption to this model of passivity: the political mobilization of women. The puzzle raised above of why there was historically little autonomous expression of women's politically related occupational demands can be easily answered. First, women, as guardians of the family, the non-work sphere, were for long less inclined than men to shape their political outlook with reference to the workplace. They participated less in organizations of all kinds, except the church. For complex reasons that need not concern us here, in most European countries it has been conservative parties that have stood for these domestic and religious interests. Although large numbers of women have joined the workforce during the past thirty years, the majority have done so part-time, so their particular connection to the domestic sphere has not been disturbed.

Second, while men, as the gender already active in public life, could set up unions and movements without anyone at the time regarding their male character as embodying some kind of attack on the female sex, for women – organizing as such after men are already organized – the situation is very different. To articulate a feminine vision is to criticize a masculine one. Given that the majority of people relate to their wider society through their families, it is difficult for women to develop the specific interests of their distinctive occupational groups without causing domestic tension and with little hope of forming communities. It is no coincidence that specifically feminist organizations usually articulate the concerns of single women more effectively than they do those of married ones.

However, since the early 1970s this situation has begun to change. There has been a mobilization, or rather a diversity of mobilizations, of female identities and their political expression. Alongside the green movement, these have constituted the most important new instances of democratic politics at work in its positive, creative sense. The development has followed the classic pattern of popular mobilizations. Starting with small groups of intellectuals and extremists, it spread to express itself in complex, rich and uncontrollable ways, but all rooted in the fundamental requirement of a great movement: the discovery of an unexpressed identity, leading to the definition of interests and the formation of formal and informal groups to give expression to these. As with all great movements, it took the existing political system by surprise and could not be easily manipulated. It also developed in ways beyond the control of official feminist movements. Feminist pioneers might not have had phenomena like Girl Power in mind when they sought to mobilize their sisters, but it is characteristic of a true major social movement that it takes a confusing and sometimes contradictory multiplicity of forms.

All the major ingredients of a great democratic phenomenon have been present: extremist radicals; sober reformist policy-makers; cunning reactionaries taking the movement's messages and reinterpreting them; both elite and popular cultural manifestations of many kinds; the gradual suffusion into the conversation of ordinary people of elements of the language of an initially esoteric movement. Gradually too the political system started to respond and produce policies addressed to women's expressed concerns in a diversity of ways. Parallel to this ran an interest of political and business elites themselves in increasing female labour-force participation. The oddly poised and possibly unstable state of contemporary gender relations, where it seems to be widely assumed that both men and women will have jobs, but women will still be the main domestic carers, makes women ideal candidates for accepting part-time work; this suits the needs of firms for a flexible workforce. And governments are also grateful for the increase in the number of taxpayers which female labour-force participation brings. But far from diminishing the importance of the movement, this only reinforces it. After all, the political rise of the manual working class was similarly accompanied by the growing dependence of the economy on its consumption power.

The capacity for political autonomy of women continues to be restrained by the factors mentioned above, but the whole experience has constituted a democratic moment within the overall framework of the onward march of post-democracy, reminding us that major historical tendencies can be contradicted.

The problem of contemporary reformism

The position of the so-called 'reformist' groups in many centre-left parties – Third Way, New Labour, *Neue Mitte, riformisti* – can easily be understood from the perspective of the foregoing discussion. Their parties' former social base had become associated with defensive decline and defeat, and no longer provided a viable launching point for ensuring contact with future-oriented development either within the electorate or on substantive issues. The organizations which were supposed to ground the politicians in the concerns of the people – the parties themselves and their associated trade unions – became increasingly detached from growth points in the electorate and in the workforce, and gave misleading signals concerning the political priorities of the new mass population of post-industrial society.

A special place is occupied in this history by New Labour in the UK. As noted above, the British manual working class, once the base of one of the most powerful labour movements in the world, had suffered particularly traumatic defeats during the early 1980s. Party and unions lurched hopelessly to the left precisely as the old base for left-wing politics was collapsing. From this experience emerged a new party leadership which was determined more than anything else to dissociate itself from its recent past. But this strategy has left the party with little in terms of distinctive social interests – with the highly significant exception of giving considerably greater attention than its Conservative and Labour predecessors to issues of importance to women, which is what the immediately preceding discussion should lead us to expect. This apart, the shift from Labour to New Labour can be read as the shift from a party suited to democratic politics to one prepared for post-democracy, through the nightmare transition of the 1980s as the democratic model ceased to be viable.

This has left the party leadership free gradually to leave its base and become a party for all. And this has been extremely successful. With the exception of the Swedish SAP, the British Labour Party has the strongest record of electoral success of any European party originating from the centre-left in recent years. (It should, however, be noted that much of this success is a product of the British electoral system, which makes difficult the organization of dissatisfaction with a party leadership, and also brings exaggerated levels of parliamentary success to a party coming first among a group of parties in terms of the popular vote.)

But for a party to have no particular base is to exist in a vacuum. That is something which political nature abhors, and the newly confident corporate interests, embodied in the newly aggressive and flexible model of the share value-maximizing firm, have rushed to fill it. This explains the paradox of New Labour in government. Here was a new, refreshing, modernizing force, oriented to change; but as its social and economic policy agenda emerged, it increasingly became a continuation of the preceding eighteen years of neo-liberal Conservative government.

That British New Labour has begun to move beyond the rapprochement and co-operation with business interests which is essential to all social democratic parties to becoming more or less a business party is evident at a number of points, not least the unusual relationships that came to light during 1998, linking many ministers, their advisers, firms of professional lobbyists who charge companies for access to ministers, and companies themselves. To the extent that some of these activities are concerned with finding sources of party funds from the business world to replace trade union funding, they relate very directly to Labour's dilemma of seeking an alternative social base to the working class. The consequences are emerging at a number of points, joining the discussion of this chapter to that of the political rise of the corporate elite discussed in the previous one, and to the changes in the internal structure of political parties to be discussed in the next chapter.

New Labour remains an extreme case among the reformists within centre-left parties in Europe, both because it has gone so far in this direction and because it has enjoyed considerable electoral success, making it the envy of many of its sister parties. But the trend is more generally shared; indeed, in terms of seeking party funds from business interests in rather dubious ways, New Labour probably has cleaner hands than its equivalents in Belgium, France or Germany. In policy terms, if the *Neue Mitte* tendency of the German SPD or the *riformisti* within the Italian Democratici della Sinistra have not moved so far as New Labour towards an agenda uncritical of business, it is because they continue to have to make a bigger compromise with trade unions and other components of industrial society. It is *not* because they have found a formula for representing the critical interests of the new post-industrial subordinate working population.

Meanwhile, a potential radical and democratic agenda remains unused. In the more purely market-oriented societies to which we are moving, income inequality, relative and even absolute poverty increase sharply. The new flexible labour markets make life very insecure for at least the bottom third of the working population. While the decline of manual work in manufacturing industry and coal-mining has reduced the proportion of work which is dirty and dangerous, much of the new service sector employment brings its own degradations. In particular, work in the rapidly growing personal services sector frequently involves a subordination of the person to employers and customers that has reintroduced many humiliating features of the old world of domestic service.

Modern work problems are not just confined to the bottom third. Throughout the occupational structure people are finding that their jobs are taking up more and more of their lives and bringing them unreasonable stress. The downsizing processes engaged in by most public- and private-sector organizations in recent years to cut staff costs have produced excessive workloads at many levels. For a large number of employees, working hours have been rising. Since both men and women now work within the formal economy, there is less overall time for leisure and family life. This is happening in an age when parents need to devote increasing energy to steering their sons and daughters through a more and more difficult childhood. Pressures from various forms of deviance, and from those areas of capitalism which have discovered that children are exceptionally soft touches as customers, compete with an frenzied need to do well educationally in order to keep one's nose in front of an occupational race which is increasing both its rewards to winners and its punishments to losers. The inadequacies of public employees by no means represent the main source of politically relevant dissatisfaction that the current political consensus represents them to be.

Politicians might argue that it has become increasingly difficult for the state to meet needs for protection from the market's vagaries, given the apparent reluctance of modern populations to pay taxes. But to argue that objectively these needs no longer exist, or could not be turned into issues of political concern by a political party seriously wanting to highlight them, is quite specious. The problems we experience at work remain high on any objective political agenda. And such an agenda could bring together new and old sections of the workforce. A party really seeking to represent the interest of these combined groups does not have far to look.

It did seem for several years that the Dutch Labour Party had found such a formula, in the successful combination of labour flexibility alongside redefined rights which has helped produce the Dutch employment 'miracle' of recent years (Visser and Hemerijck 1997). The defeat of that party and its coalition partners in the first 2002 election, which so strongly featured the temporary triumph of the Lijst Pim Fortuyn, was therefore a highly disturbing development. It can be explained by the fact that the party had never been able to develop the new Dutch employment strategy as a partisan policy fighting for the interests of certain newly defined employee groups – though in practice that is what it was doing. The policy was developed – and for strategic reasons probably had to be developed – as a class compromise, consensus policy stretching across the political spectrum. As such, therefore, it could play little role in boldly articulating a new employee interest, but probably instead contributed to the general sense of Dutch voters that their ruling politicians had become sunk in compromise, leading so many of them to seek the new 'clarity' that Fortuyn and his associates were promising. In the absence of any articulation of new class-rooted interests, these clear identities took almost the only available alternative form: identity of nation and race against newcomers from ethnic minorities.

Several other notable cases of social democratic electoral defeat during the 1990s by governing parties with good practical records on issues important to working people, manual and non-manual alike, can be explained in similar ways. Austrian and Danish social democrats had, like the Dutch, developed their new progressive policies within coalitions with some of their main rivals. French socialists were in cohabitation with a centre-right president. The Ulivo coalition in Italy was unable to sustain its own tensions between left and centre parties, quarrels among whom became more prominent than any policy agenda. In each case, a good new agenda of employment policy was being developed; but in each case this could not contribute to a process of new identity-building, because it had been formed within a government consensus and not in political struggle.

The greater success of Swedish social democrats in their national elections of 2002 reinforces the argument, as this was a government which had made some progress on an agenda of this kind but without needing to form coalitions with parties representing very different interests. The narrow survival of the red–green coalition in Germany demonstrates something else. This government had done little to adopt an employment agenda of the Dutch or French kind, but Germany retains a higher (though declining) proportion of industrial employment than most other advanced societies. Reform is therefore less pressing. However, this situation will not last much longer, and German social democracy will soon be forced to face the choices of post-industrial politics.

Meanwhile a point of major significance is that, in each of the cases where the forces of the centre-left were trapped by coalition or cohabitation obligations from trying to develop and mobilize new partisan social identities favourable to themselves, parties representing nationalistic, anti-immigrant or racist politics – clear, uncompromising identities – made gains, though often very temporary ones, in the context of the centre-left's defeat. The temporary character of most of these suggests that racism as such was less important than a popular desire for a politics which seems to address people's concerns from outside the framework of established political and social elites.

4

The Political Party under Post-Democracy

Political science textbooks usually model the relationship between parties and their wider electorates in terms of a series of related circles of growing size: the smallest comprises the leadership core, together with its advisers; next come parliamentary representatives; then active members, people who spend a lot of their time working actively for the party, as local government representatives, local activists, paid staff; next, ordinary members, who do little for the party, but want to have a symbolic attachment to it, help with the occasional activity, and pay a regular membership subscription; then supporters, or loyal voters, who do virtually nothing for the party except reliably turn out for it on election days; finally, the largest circle of all, the wider target electorate, which the party seeks to persuade to vote for it.

In the pure model of a democratic party these circles are concentric: the leaders are drawn from the activists, who are drawn from the party membership, which is part of and therefore reflects the concerns and interests of those parts of the electorate which the party most seeks to represent. A major function of the intermediate circles is to link political leaders to the electorate in a two-way interaction via the various levels of the party.

This type of model is particularly important to the self-image of working-class parties, as well as those that are regionalist and separatist parties, and some that are Christian Democratic and fascist. Such parties originated outside parliament as social movements and then developed a parliamentary arm. During the course of the twentieth century, however, social roots became increasingly important also for older parties which had originated within the political elite and subsequently cast about to fabricate for themselves a national movement as the age of democracy crept up on them. Ironically these parties have increasingly presented themselves as movement parties in precisely the period when the advance of post-democracy makes their earlier model as a disembodied political elite more realistic.

Like all ideals, the democratic model of concentric circles never really exists. However, there can be movement towards or away from it at different times, and it is instructive to observe these. Tensions occur within any organization basically resembling the democratic model when the leadership suspects that the activists are a very biased sample of even the loyal electorate; since they are self-selected, this is likely to be true. It can then be expected to use other methods of discovering voters' views. Until the mid-twentieth century and the invention of mass opinion polling this was difficult to do, and it was during this period that active members were able to establish their claim to interpret the voters' stances. Today matters are very different.

Tensions become even greater when leaderships believe that the support base provided by the loyal electorate is too small, and start casting around for votes in the pool of the general electorate. If this involves approaching groups alien to the concerns of the activists, and in no way concentric to the existing party, there will be conflict. If there is success in getting some of the new groups within the active membership, then the conflict takes place among activists themselves, but the party has been constructively renewed. If the new groups are tapped only by opinion polling and other non-membership methods, there is the possibility of a curious bond linking the innermost and outermost of the concentric circles, at the expense of all intermediate relationships.

The challenge of post-democracy

Recent changes, including those discussed in previous chapters concerning the rise of the firm and the confusion of class structure, have had major implications for the concentric model. A further change has been the vast extension of circles of advisers and lobbyists around leaderships. Although three groups can be distinguished – leaders, advisers and lobbyists – in practice individuals move between these positions, and together comprise the specialized occupation of politics.

This process changes the shape of the leadership core in relation to the other party circles. It becomes an ellipse. This begins where it always did, with party leaders and activist professionals at the heart of the party, seeking as reward either advancement into the leadership or the psychic rewards of policy success. But there are also those who, even though sympathetic to the party and its goals, work for it primarily for money. Beyond them are pure professionals, who are hired by the party to do a job, and who may not necessarily be its political supporters. More important, all these groups overlap and interact with groups of lobbyists working for firms who have an interest in government business to establish contacts with politicians. As discussed in chapter 2 and as will be seen in more detail in chapter 5, a party in or eligible for government today is heavily involved in privatization and sub-contracting. Links with government personnel can be vital for firms wanting to gain from this. Sub-contracting is the more important, because it usually relates to services close to the heart of policy, therefore unable to be fully privatized, and with contracts subject to periodic renewal. Firms wanting a share of this business are well advised to maintain permanent contact with the policy-making core of a governing party. Members of the firms spend periods within the advisory circles, and party advisers get jobs as lobbyists with the firms. In this the inner core become stretched from being an inner circle of the party to being an ellipse stretching way out beyond the party's ranks.

All parties experience this vulnerability. It lies behind many of the corruption scandals that have affected parties of all colours in today's advanced societies. Once the concept of what makes public service special has been held up to ridicule and cynicism, and the pursuit of personal profit has been elevated into the supreme human goal, it can only be expected that politicians, advisers and others will regard selling their political influence for gain as a major and totally legitimate aspect of their participation in political life. But the general problem of the elliptical political elite presents special difficulties for social democratic parties, as their membership and electoral cores are that much further removed from elites than are those of right-of-centre parties. Particularly problematic for them have been the consequences of the post-1980s changes in class structure discussed in chapter 3. As the manual working class shrank in size, party activists who looked largely to that class became of diminishing use as links between leadership and wider electorate. The leadership naturally sought to escape being caught in this historical trap, and turned increasingly to expert channels for advice on public opinion. While tensions of this kind are endemic to the concentric model, at a period of major class change they can become unmanageable. The processes used to discover the opinions of new groups were top-down and passive; very little resulted from autonomous mobilization by the groups themselves. And the result of the use of experts was to move the structure of the leadership further from the circles of the party towards the ellipse.

The main historical value of activists to party leaderships has been their contribution to vote gathering, either directly through their unremunerated time, or through financial contributions and fund-raising. The new extended ellipse tries to provide its own partial alternatives to this too. The firms which increasingly congregate around party leaderships can offer a party money that can be used in the national, and particularly television, campaigns that have largely replaced local activities for vote gathering.

From the point of view of a party leadership, relations with the new ellipse are much easier, better informed and more rewarding than those with the old circles of activists. The expertise of the ellipse is of far more use than the amateur enthusiasm that is all that the normal party activist has to offer. If we extrapolate from recent trends, the classic party of the twenty-first century would be one which comprises a self-reproducing inner elite, remote from its mass movement base, but nested squarely within a number of corporations, which will in turn fund the sub-contracting of opinion-polling, policy-advice and vote-gathering services, in exchange for firms that seek political influence being well regarded by the party when in government.

At present only one almost pure example of such a party exists, and it is a party of the right, not of social democracy: Forza Italia in Italy. Following the collapse through corruption scandals of the Christian Democratic and Socialist Parties in the early 1990s, the entrepreneur Silvio Berlusconi – who had in fact been closely associated with the old regime – rapidly filled the vacuum which would otherwise have ensured an easy passage to government by the then Communist Party by pooling resources from his extensive network of enterprises. These comprised: television channels, a publishing house, a major football club, a financial empire, a leading supermarket chain, and so on. Within a matter of months he had established one of the leading parties in the Italian state, and, despite various vicissitudes largely resulting from corruption scandals, it has remained so. Initially Forza Italia had no members or activists at all as such. Many of the functions normally filled by volunteers were carried out by the employees of Berlusconi's various enterprises. External funding was obviously not needed, and a man who owns three national television channels, a national newspaper and a popular weekly magazine does not need party activists to get his message across.

Forza Italia is an example of a political party produced by the forces identified in chapter 2: it is essentially a firm, or network of firms, rather than an organization of the classic party type; it did not emerge from any formulation of interests by social groups, but was a construction built up by parts of the existing political and financial elite. It is also based on the personality of its leader more than on any particular party programme. As noted in chapter 1, this is itself highly characteristic of post-democracy.

However, the story of Forza Italia also shows us that the time is by no means yet fully ripe for a party totally of this new kind. As the years have passed, so it has come to resemble more closely a classic party: it has acquired members and a local voluntary structure, and it has become more successful as a result. The crucial element here has been the importance in Italy of local government as the prime link between people and politics and as the lifeblood of parties. Forza Italia had to acquire local bases and actual members in order to have an actual and not just a virtual presence among the electorate, both day-to-day and for getting the vote out at election time. As it did this it started to achieve success in local politics to match its national presence – though partly by Berlusconi using his television stations to turn local elections into little more than a reflection of national politics.

That dispensing with party activists is premature can also be seen from the experience of New Labour. The party has made a major and successful effort to attract corporate funding to replace dependency on trade unions and the mass membership. However, the new form of politics, with its reliance on extremely heavy mass media presentations and purchased professional services, is very expensive. The party's needs for money have become enormous. Millionaires have not *replaced* members or trade unions, because New Labour cannot afford to dispense with any kinds of funds now that elections have become so costly. But the actions necessary to attract new, wealthy business donors may well deter these other types of supporter.

One of the factors behind the recent rise in political corruption scandals among parties of all types in a number of countries, including Belgium, France, Germany, Italy, Japan and Spain, has been this vast appetite for funds to feed contemporary election campaigns. It would be a foolhardy party that would try to shift away from dependence on members and unions to dependence on corporations, when it might instead receive money from both. Ironically, the very cost of professionalized electioneering sends parties back to the arms of the traditional activists, and at the same time tempts them into dubious practices. At present, all these forces co-exist uneasily and in mutual suspicion.

It was argued in the opening chapter that the post-democratic period combines characteristics of the democratic and pre-democratic periods as well as those distinctly its own. This is the case with the contemporary political party. The legacy of the democratic model survives and continues to play a vital part, though without much capacity to renew itself, in the continuing dependence of leaders on the circles of the traditional mass party. The new ellipse running from the leadership through its consultants to external lobbies paradoxically constitutes both the post-democratic and pre-democratic part. It is post-democratic in so far as it is concerned with the opinion research and expert policy work characteristic of this period. It is pre-democratic in the way that it provides privileged political access for individual firms and commercial interests. The tensions within the contemporary party of the centre-left are the tensions of post-democracy itself. The fact that new classes have not been mobilized creates a curious mix of old constituencies and new money.

5

Post-Democracy and the Commercialization of Citizenship

The ideas and realities of public services and the welfare state that developed during the twentieth century were a fundamental part of the democratization of politics. Sometimes, as most clearly in the Scandinavian cases, they were the direct achievement of the democratic struggle. Elsewhere, as in Germany before the First World War, they were instituted as palliatives to dilute the pressure for democracy. But everywhere they had something to do with that struggle. And as democracy settled down into the second half of the twentieth century the quality of public services became fundamental to the character and quality of social citizenship. Throughout the advanced capitalist world, the model of the citizenship state existed alongside a vigorous market sector. The relationship between the social state and the market zone was always complex and varied considerably among countries, but almost everywhere there was some concept that the serious business of social citizenship needed somehow to be distanced from market competition and profit. That assumption was fundamental to the idea of democratic citizenship, because this implied a system of distribution and decision-making that did not embody the inequalities of the capitalist component of society. The tension between the egalitarian demands of democracy and the inequalities that result from capitalism can never be resolved, but there can be more or less constructive compromises around it.

Today these assumptions are seriously challenged, and the increasingly powerful lobbies of business interests ask why public services and welfare policies should not be available to them for profit-making purposes just like everything else. We accept commercial restaurants and barbers, why not schools and health services? Are there really good grounds for being concerned at the commercialization of welfare? And does the debate over privatization have anything to do with the problem of post-democracy? This requires some analysis.

Attempts at marrying what have until now been primarily public services with capitalist practices take a variety of forms: markets within public ownership; privatization with or without fully free markets; contracting out both capital projects and service delivery, sometimes without either privatization or markets. The relationship of the market to private ownership is more ambiguous than is often assumed. Certainly perfect markets alongside private ownership of economic resources provide the conditions for the capitalism of economics textbooks, and the two criteria fit together well. It is, however, entirely possible to have markets without private ownership: an authority owning collective resources can decide to use a system of prices and tokens in order to make a market through which to allocate these resources within a public or charitable service. This idea informed many welfare state reforms of the 1980s, especially in the UK, which were often precursors of actual privatization. Government departments and service units were required to trade services with other units as though they were in a market relationship, abandoning the professional colleague model that had previously governed their interactions. A major example was the internal market introduced into the National Health Service.

The generic term which will be used here for all these practices is commercialization, because each is premised on the assumption that the quality of public services will be improved if the existing practices and ethos of public service are partially replaced by those typical of commercial practice. This concept is more accurate than marketization, for some of the processes now being introduced involve distortions of the market rather than its purification. And it is more general than privatization, which, strictly speaking, refers only to the transfer of ownership assets.

Capitalism had its greatest achievements and its dominance with industrialization. The enlarged production of material goods which this made possible released the spiral between investment in plant and equipment, production and sale of a good and further investment of the proceeds from these sales which became the great engine of nineteenth- and twentieth-century wealth and prosperity. But capitalism expands its scope not just by developing new goods and production methods, but also by energetically pulling more and more areas of life within its reach. Through the process usually known as commodification, human activities existing outside the market and the system of accumulation are brought within their ambit. And this can apply to services just as much as the production of material goods. Indeed, capitalism originated in postmedieval Europe in services sectors, mainly banking, and in recent decades these have again become fundamental to it – another parabolic development.

Capitalism can extend its reach if services that might have been rendered as, say, a community or family obligation are transformed into wage labour and sold. Much of the political conflict of the previous two centuries concerned the boundaries which a great diversity of other interests – for example, churches, the working class – sought to erect around the rampaging force of capitalism trying to bring more and more areas of life within its grasp (Crouch 1999a: ch. 1). Various compromises were eventually established: Sundays and other religious holidays were more or less protected from the capitalist working week; family life remained uncommodified, mainly through the withdrawal of the majority of married women from the labour market; various limits were imposed on the exploitation of labour; and by the mid-twentieth century a series of basic services were at least partly removed from the reach of capitalism and the market because their provision was considered too important and universal. As T.H. Marshall (1963) memorably argued, people acquired rights to these goods and services, mainly the latter, by virtue of their status as citizens, and not because they were able to buy them in the market. Just as it became a mark of democracy that the right to vote or to a fair trial was not available for market purchase, so entitlement to certain services became a similar mark; provision of them through market means would demean their citizenship quality. (In most capitalist societies the idea that legal and democratic rights are untouched by the market has in fact remained a myth. Rich people and groups can hire superior lawyers, and supplement their democratic rights by lobbying power. However, the rhetorical moral appeal of equality before the law and in the ballot box is unchallenged.) These services were not necessarily delivered free of charge, but any charges were notional, and designed explicitly not to be used as rationing or allocation devices.

The list of items included has varied across societies and over time, but usually includes entitlement to certain levels of education, health care, certain forms of care service (including various kinds of child support) in case of need, and financial support in old age and in the event of temporary or permanent loss of earning capacity through unemployment, ill health or injury.

Although conflicts over these exclusions from the reach of commodification and the market were often bitter and difficult, the task of those trying to restrict the reach of capitalism within social life was made easier by the fact that for most of the period the best opportunities for profit and extending the scope of the market lay in industrial production. This process received a particular boost in the years around the Second World War, the democratic moment of most of the western world, when the exigencies of increasingly technological warfare gave an exogenous stimulus to invention, research and development in many fields, with manifold subsequent peacetime uses. It was as western capitalism was relaxing into enjoying these possibilities that important compromises over labour rights and the welfare state were negotiated. By the late 1960s and early 1970s this process had peaked. The same processes that have been seen at other points in these pages having a major effect on the parabola of democracy were here again at work.

While innovations in the production of goods have still continued apace, major new developments have required increasingly costly research and large-scale investment. At the same time many new opportunities began to open in the provision to an increasingly wealthy population of services rather than goods: new forms of distribution, increasing travel, new forms of financial and other business services, growing use of restaurants and other food outlets, more interest in taking advantage of health, education, legal and other professional services. Increasingly, capitalist firms have sought their profits in these sectors as well as, and gradually instead of, manufacturing.

But this has raised a problem. Some of these services, potentially very profitable ones and of widespread interest, are those of the welfare state, protected from private ownership and the market alike as part of the mid-century citizenship package. So long as the welfare state survives, potential areas of profit-making are excluded from capital's reach. Post-industrial capitalism has therefore started to try to undo the deals made by its industrial predecessor and tear down the barriers to commercialization and commodification imposed by mid-twentieth century concepts of citizenship. They are powerfully aided in this by the World Trade Organization (WTO), which has been charged by the governments of the world's most powerful countries with liberalizing the international exchange of goods and services. It has no other responsibilities and recognizes no other human priorities; it is an institution born during the growing tide of post-democracy, and has a thoroughly post-democratic set of responsibilities.

The only right it protects against open competition is the right of patent, hence its support – until a major political issue was created around the practice – of multinational pharmaceuticals firms in preventing poor countries from marketing cheap, competitive forms of vital medicines. In addition to liberalizing existing markets, the WTO tries to introduce markets into fields that have previously been governed by different principles. It has in particular identified the welfare state, including state education and health services, as areas that should be opened up to markets, or to privatization (Hatcher 2000; Price, Pollock and Shaoul 1999). As a result of these pressures, almost everywhere the content of the citizenship package has come under attack.

Citizenship and markets

An essential starting point for a critique of this pressure for commercialization is the observation that the maximization of markets and private ownership can conflict with other human goals. While the WTO has neither the will nor the mandate to consider these, individual governments, organizations and private persons are free to place markets into perspective and to debate whether or not they should be accepted uncritically as the sole criterion to govern our affairs. To try to prevent this debate from taking place is to place a major constraint on the capacity of democracy. Almost no-one except a tiny number of extreme libertarians would disagree with this in principle. For example, virtually no conservatives (or anyone else) believe that sexual relationships, or those between parents and children, should be forced into a market frame. Virtually no conservatives and not many liberals would argue that national political sovereignty should be capable of being traded in the market, or that the ability of people to change their residence from country to country should be governed only by labour-market opportunities and not by state immigration policy.

The market is not capable of being an absolute principle, a categorical imperative, since it is a means for achieving ends and not an end in itself. The case for the market is that if we follow its rules we shall make allocation decisions that better reach our goals, whatever these goals are. Other means of making allocations always remain suspect to the doubt that they do not provide as efficient a means of calculating costs, including opportunity costs, as the actual market. But this does not dispose of two principal points: that the market can fail to register all relevant elements of a choice of good; and that its use can itself change negatively the quality of a good. The former criticism is of major practical importance, but it is at least capable of being remedied by improving the quality of the market itself, rather than by suppressing it. For example, if the price of a good fails to represent the costs of pollution created in its production, it is possible to impose a tax reflecting the cost of the pollution, which will then be reflected in the price.

The second objection, that use of the market per se negatively changes the sought good itself, is more fundamental. For example, most people consider that sexual relationships offered under conditions of prostitution are inherently inferior to non-marketed ones. Prostitution could doubtless be improved if its market were made more perfect: for example, if it were subject to no legal prohibitions, the level of exploitation it involved and its sordid conditions of service delivery would be alleviated. But that is not the main point of the objection, which relates to an absolute judgement of quality.

Can objections of this kind be considered to apply in the field of citizenship services? The issue turns on two principal problems that can be caused by the application of commercial principles: distortion and residualization.

Distortion

Providing goods or services through markets involves an elaborate procedure of creating barriers of access so that we cannot get them without payment. Sometimes the character of a good itself has to be changed to do this. We accept these distortions or most goods and services would not be provided at all; most obviously, traders would not be willing to set up shops if we did not accept cash desks and the whole procedure of money exchange.

There are instances, however, where the extent of distortion required so damages the quality of the good in question or erects barriers so artificial that one may reasonably doubt whether the gains from any efficiency improvement are worth the losses incurred: for example, when entrepreneurs are allowed to buy pieces of coastline and charge for access to beaches or cliff walks. Another example is the interruption of television programmes by the advertisements that are needed to fund their production.

A more specific example was provided by the record of the Child Support Agency, set up in the UK by the Conservative government of the 1980s to increase contributions to children's maintenance from parents (usually fathers) who were no longer supporting their former partners in the children's up-bringing. As a product of the neo-liberal approach to government, the Agency was not concerned with pursuing justice and even-handedness as in an elementary citizenship model of legal rights. Its task was to operate like a private debt-collection firm, and its staff had financial incentives to maximize the returns to government revenue that they could achieve. Therefore the Agency found it easier to demand more money from fathers already making some payment, and therefore easy to trace, than to track down those making no contribution at all. Seen in terms of the ideals of justice and even-handedness among citizens, this was a distortion of purpose and the agency was widely unpopular and regarded with lack of trust. But seen from the perspective of good business principles, the Agency was taking the right steps to maximize its returns. Principles of justice become distorted when subordinated to those of business.

Another form of distortion occurs when artificial attempts are made to provide indicators that can serve as the analogues of prices, particularly in the shadow markets which are often used within public services to avoid some of the problems of privatization while securing important advantages of markets. Where markets are virtual and goods and services are not really traded, there is a strong temptation to use as an indicator those elements that can be easily measured, rather than the qualities of the good or service really at stake. Service providers are likely to concentrate on those aspects of their work which are included in the indicators, neglecting others, not because they are intrinsically less important but because they are less measurable. In the UK the New Labour government's attempts to benchmark reduction of certain waiting lists for medical treatment have produced several such distortions: health service managers and professionals concentrate resources on those items being assessed and made politically prominent by drawing off resources from other, less easily observed, parts of the service. The apparent efficiency gains of this kind of targeting can become quite illusory; if, as may well be the case, the easily measured items are not in fact the most important, there may even be a loss of real effectiveness. This can be tackled by increasing the number of indicators, but that eventually leads to measurement overload and excessive complexity.

The value of an indicator depends on its ability to measure accurately the quality that the customer is seeking, and this can be in doubt, even in 'real' markets. Stock-exchange evaluations of companies often present biased and distorted estimates of a firm's long-term worth; the exchange rates of currencies often bear only a poor relationship to their respective purchasing power; relative incomes are not the only legitimate means of comparing the value of two occupations. The problem intensifies in the case of shadow or artificial markets, as in public-service applications. Here the indicator is typically chosen by a political or administrative authority and not by users, with the result that they are likely to suit political or managerial criteria rather than the client sensitivity which is in principle a major objective of the exercise. In the stock-exchange-led form of capitalism that became dominant by the end of the twentieth century, this problem of indicators ceased to be a matter of concern. As was seen with a large number of information technology firms, which had very high share values before they ever sold a product to a customer, the value of a firm's shares became entirely self-justifying: if enough people believe that the share value is an indicator of something import-ant, they will buy the shares and the value will have justified itself (Castells 1996: ch. 2). Such an economy is vulnerable to sudden collapses of confidence when these houses of cards collapse; but the process of rebuilding soon gets under way again.

This type of economy is also highly vulnerable to corruption, as became clear during the US accounting scandals discussed earlier. While such practices were widely condemned, they could in fact be defended in the terms that the so-called 'new economy' had established during the 1990s. If the value of an economic activity is seen as residing solely in the value of its shares, and if share values are 'real' provided enough investors believe them to be real and therefore buy the shares, then what is wrong in trying to kick-start a collapsed confidence by pretending that profits have been earned? Provided enough people believe this to be real, the share price will grow again, and the self-justifying process will have started again.

A similar logic to all this is at work in the use of indica-tors to measure achievements in welfare state services. If people believe that the indicators measure something real, then they will feel better when they learn that scores measured by indicators have improved. And if they feel better, they will reward the government that has produced the good results. In the process sight has been lost of the actual state of the services, unless and until some awkward critics succeed in attracting attention back to these. In the meantime there has been a major distortion of perspectives.

Residualization

The market is often depicted as a realm of consumer sovereignty: firms can sell their goods and services only if we choose to buy them. But it is providers who initially choose their customers, by deciding on which segments of the market they wish to target their products. There can be no obligation on any firm to try to meet everyone's needs. Public services differ fundamentally from this, in that they *must* be universal in their potential scope. Private–public partnership in such provision means allowing the private providers to choose the segments they want, while the public service guarantees provision for those in whom the private sector has no interest. Such public provision is residual, and we know both in theory and in practice from the works of scholars like Albert Hirschman (1970) and Richard Titmuss (1970) that residual public services becomes services of poor quality, because only the poor and politically ineffective have to make use of them.

Matters become even worse when public services are *required* to have residual status and degraded quality because government is deliberately making space for commercial provision. This can easily happen when governments are desperate to privatize in order to improve their cash balances with the proceeds of the sale. Such services are then excluded from the realms of both markets and citizenship. Public services of this kind cannot be described as 'citizenship': access to them is more a penalty than a right; and the essential citizenship mechanism of voice must not be made available to residual recipients or they might seek improvements that would break the rule of no competition with market provision.

An important example may be taken from the world of employment placement and unemployment assistance. The logic of a neo-liberal market regime is to privatize as much employment placement as possible, leaving a public service to deal with the hard-to-place, the unemployed. The administration of unemployment benefit must therefore be joined to sanctions on them concerning the kinds of jobs they must take. They lose both market choice – they do not have the requirements for market entry – and citizenship, as they are now in a world where benefit withdrawal may be threatened, and not one where security is a right. During the 1960s and 1970s it was generally considered in advanced countries that state employment services should provide as extensive a service as possible, and that the administration of public assistance should be separated from a placement service, as the aim of placement was seen – in both efficiency and citizenship terms – as being to maximize individuals' opportunities for suitable and fulfilling work. The current orthodoxy is exactly the opposite: privatization is required in European Union countries under the Treaty of Amsterdam and generally encouraged by the Organization for Economic Co-operation and Development. Also required is the re-amalgamation of placement and assistance services and a shift from provision of a right for citizens in difficulties to cajoling the unemployed into finding some kind of work by making life as unemployed very unattractive. Desmond King (1995) has shown the negative implications that this can have for quality of service for the poor unemployed in an analysis of how these changes have affected the operation of the British and US employment services.

The degradation of markets

It has already been pointed out that there can be resort to private ownership or a contribution from private providers without marketization of the service concerned, especially if by market we understand the pure market of economics textbooks. This requires a very large number (tending to infinity) of competing producers and customers, with low barriers to entry by new producers. The regulatory system must also confine itself to maintaining the conditions of perfect competition, and must offer absolutely no favours or privileges to individual producers or customers. These stringent conditions fulfil two purposes. First, they ensure the lowest possible prices consistent with keeping producers in the market: under perfect competition every producer is a price taker; no-one is in a position to fix or even influence prices by their individual action. Second, the condition of anonymity that this condition and the requirement of no privileged access to the regulatory authority impose means that there can be no political interference to favour individual producers over others. Indeed, in neo-classical economics there is no scope at all for lobbying the regulatory authority on behalf of producer interests – unless one permits requests for regulatory change submitted openly and on behalf of all producers in the market.

There are many goods and services where something like these conditions are fulfilled, but it is obviously not true of those where it is difficult to sustain large numbers of firms. Recent economic theory and the assumptions increasingly used by competition authorities have compromised with the often unrealistic nature of the conditions of perfect competition for oligopolistic sectors. It has been noted that very small numbers of giant firms can in fact compete very keenly indeed with each other on price; therefore oligopolies in sectors like petrol, and sheer monopoly in computer software, are not considered to offend against anti-trust regulations. However, this assumes that only price is of interest. It ignores the important political concerns about privileged lobbying of political authorities which the stringent conditions of the pure market were also intended to address. Competition among oligopolistic firms does not necessarily imply a diminution in privileged political lobbying and may even enhance it, as these firms use political measures as part of their competitive struggle. For eighteenth-century political economists, in particular Adam Smith, as well as such twentieth-century successors as Friedrich von Hayek, the guarantee of anonymity and the incapacity of any individual producer to affect conditions by itself were important for these political reasons. Smith would certainly not have regarded the political role of such companies as Enron or Microsoft as consistent with his idea of the market economy.

Smith, of course, did not have to come to terms with the reality of mass democracy, and he probably would not have fully approved of it. However, as noted in chapter 2, we know that he would certainly not have approved of the business-lobby-dominated politics of post-democracy, and may possibly have shared a realization that, in the conditions of early twenty-first-century society, only the vigilance of a reinvigorated democracy might be able to check the inefficiencies and dubious practices likely to arise from the ellipse linking a politicized business elite to a self-referential political class. Von Hayek more or less accepted democracy, but hoped that means would be found for containing its tendency to criticize the capitalist market. He never faced up to a central problem: given that, for any individual capitalist enterprise, there is more profit in having political influence than in being subject to the market, how could a political process dominated by capitalist forces avoid slipping into a set of business lobbies? The Hayekian model might work in a true neo-classical economy, where no firms have political influence, and where all might share a general political preference for a system in which means are found to ensure that no firms acquire such influence; but in the conditions of the late twentieth and early twenty-first centuries this is unrealis-tic. Large corporations have developed a political capacity and influence far in excess of those small and medium-sized enterprises who remain under the political con-straints of the true market, and they use this not only to secure their substantive ends, but also to ensure the maintenance of a political system that permits the exercise of such influence.

These problems become of fundamental importance when we address privatization and major exercises in public-service sub-contracting, for here lobbying and the development of special relationships with politicians and civil servants of the kind which very large, far from anonymous, firms can carry out become acutely relevant. Securing the privatization contract, establishing its terms and planning its eventual renewal have become occasions for intensive interaction within the ellipse of the new polit-ical class: very small numbers of elite individuals repre-senting corporations (often former ministers and civil servants), political advisers and the staff of party think tanks, and current ministers and civil servants. It is impossible to check the role of 'old pal' networks, contri-butions to party funds, promises of post-public-service directorships, etc., in these exchanges. Now that success in securing private contractors has become an important symbol of political virtue, national and local politicians may want no other reward than the willingness of a firm to accept one of their contracts – hardly an incentive for tough bargaining. In the case of full privatization, the fact that the firms involved are not perfect market agents is frequently recognized by the establishment of regulatory authorities to monitor the subsequent behaviour of the industry. There are then grounds for concern over the relationship between the regulator and the lobbyists. The claim widely made for privatization that it will depoliticize an industry or service and provide a guarantee against corruption is highly disingenuous. Far from reducing opportunities for corruption in relations between government and business, the strategy considerably increases them and produces a special class of firms with highly privileged political access. The more politically salient the service concerned, the more problematic this becomes.

Privatizing or contracting out?

The distinction between privatization and contracting out requires further analysis. Under the former, ownership of a previous public resource is transferred to private firms. Under the latter, ownership remains with the public sector, but the performance of individual parts of the service is provided by profit-seeking firms, on contracts of varying length. There is clearly a difference. For example, in privatizing railways, governments can privatize everything, or retain ownership of the railway network and contract out the provision of train, station and goods-handling services.

This distinction has become very important to 'Third Way' approaches such as that of the UK New Labour government, which insists that its strategy towards health and education involves partnerships between public and private finance and sub-contracting service delivery, not the transfer of public assets to private owners, which is defined as privatization. While this avoids the loss of ownership and ultimate control of a public asset involved in privatization, it in fact intensifies the problem at the centre of concern here: privileged lobbying and access to ministers and civil servants by individual corporations. Precisely because there is no final privatization of assets in contracting out services or in public–private financial partnerships, the relationship between public authority and private provider becomes a continuing one, and therefore the lobbying and temptations of mutual exchanges of favours become permanent. Both forms necessarily feature contracts of long duration. In the case of privately financed capital projects, like a hospital or large school, contracts have to be very long indeed, often over thirty years. Given the short lifespan of contemporary political and organizational arrangements, these are more than lifetime contracts. When services are contracted out there is not the need for such very lengthy periods, but there are still certain sunk costs and also a lengthy learning curve for the private contractor. Contracts of five to seven years are normal.

During contracts of both these typical lengths, the principal becomes very dependent on the agent for the quality of delivery. There may be penalty clauses for non-delivery, but these and performance targets can be specified only for currently foreseen needs and objectives. Contracts are legally binding documents which cannot be easily amended to take account of change; long-term contracts are a curiously rigid and inflexible instrument to be adopting during a period which is normally seen as one requiring particularly rapid adaptability and flexibility. In the case of shorter-term (five- to seven-year) service contracts, firms have to start thinking about contract renewal after a fairly short period. This certainly gives them incentives to perform well on the existing contract, but the history of contracting tells us not to be naïve. There are far easier, more targeted ways of ensuring contract renewal by cultivating good relations with a few key decision-making individuals than by performing good service delivery day after day.

It is particularly interesting to observe how a number of firms are emerging who are specialists in the general art of government contracting, and pursue contracts across a wide diversity of sectors – for example, building missile-warning systems and organizing primary school inspections, to take a real British example. Clearly a firm experienced in building missile-warning systems has no initial expertise and therefore no particular substantive value added to offer when it first seeks a contract to run some schools. What it possesses is skill in winning government contracts from politicians and civil servants; it is the skill of becoming a member of the post-democratic ellipse discussed in chapter 4. Is this necessarily a skill that passes value added and service quality to the ultimate consumers themselves? After all, the need for the skill could have been avoided simply by not bringing in the private agent at all.

The loss of the concept of public authority

Government's behaviour in relation to actual and potential private contractors, and uncritical acceptance of their participation in formulating public policies from which they will themselves benefit, are examples of the phenomenon mentioned in chapter 2: the collapse of self-confidence on the part of the state and of the meaning of public authority and public service. It is useful to remember that public service was a pre-democratic concept. In many countries it was further developed during the heyday of what we now often see as unrestrained capitalism. The explanation of the paradox is that, precisely because they were staking out the liberties of capitalism, and frequently encountering the points where these clashed with other values and interests, nineteenth-century reformers took seriously Adam Smith's concern that the business world could corrupt politics *just as much* as politics would corrupt business. Politicians and civil servants therefore needed an ethic of their own, which demanded from them conduct different from that of the business world. They frequently failed to live up to these ideals, which is why we often see the late nineteenth century as hypocritical, but the ideals were there. People in public life were expected to be very careful in their dealings with those persons who represented concentrations of business power. They were also expected to maintain some sense of a public interest that was more than the sum of individual business ambitions, or of what could be induced through such ambitions. This idea developed out of the concept of the superior interests of the monarch, but it adapted itself to bourgeois capitalism and the need for the state to become an external regulator, and then reached its apogee in the social democratic ideal of the state as the servant of the universal citizen.

Such an approach did not imply hostility to capitalist behaviour, but a recognition of its appropriate limits and of the distinctive ethic and behaviour codes of public service. Similar processes affected the position of the military and the church in their relationship to the gradually emerging civil and secular state. As political life developed institutional structures that did not rely on displays of military force, it came to be seen that political and military codes needed a mutual separation. For advocates of civilian political life to insist on this separation and on an avoidance of political involvement by the military did not mean that they were pacifists. Similarly, it was eventually possible for devout Christian politicians to insist that the roles of church and state must be kept separate.

One of the changes introduced by so-called 'new public management' within the context of neo-liberal hegemony during the 1980s was a redefinition of the boundary between government and private interests as a semi-permeable one: business can interfere with government as much as it likes, but not vice versa. Those who contest this model are criticized as being necessarily 'anti-business'. This is a very one-sided exaggeration of the political teaching of classical economics, and represents an unprincipled adaptation to the realities of business lobbying power. The intellectual rationalization it uses is the neo-liberal theory of the essential wisdom of firms and the essential idiocy of government described in chapter 2. Competitive success in a perfect market, it is argued, depends in part on having the best possible knowledge, for incorrect knowledge will lead to errors of strategy and eventual bankruptcy. Therefore successful firms can be assumed to have perfect knowledge, which includes the capacity perfectly to anticipate the actions of all other market actors. This is an axiomatic assumption, since it is assumed that in the long run the market ensures the survival of only the fittest – in this case, the firms with the best capacity for acquiring knowledge. No such assumptions can be made about government. It does not exist in a state of perfect competition; therefore its knowledge is deeply suspect.

This thesis is used, *inter alia*, to argue against all government intervention in the economy. If firms in the market necessarily have superior knowledge to government, anything government tries to persuade them to do will be less efficient than what they are doing already. In fact, given their capacity for perfect anticipation, firms will have already worked out what government will be trying to achieve by its intervention and taken evasive action. This perfect knowledge is seen as residing in particular in firms that have achieved successful survival in the financial markets, who deal specifically in economic knowledge, and whose judgement should therefore never be challenged.

The argument has three practical weaknesses. First, since very many markets are far from perfect, it cannot be assumed that even the most successful firms have honed their knowledge-gathering capacities to the highest possible degree. Second, in a rapidly changing world, we cannot ever specify what will actually constitute perfect knowledge after the immediate future; since knowledge acquisition takes time, we cannot assume that any firm has enough knowledge to deal with the longer-term future. During the extended stock-market boom of the 1990s many normally thoughtful people came to believe that somehow the information technology sector had finally solved all such problems. The collapse of that boom since 2000 should serve as a valuable reminder that the knowledge embedded in stock exchanges can be less than perfect. Third, certain forms of knowledge are peculiarly available to centrally located agents (i.e. governments), who are able to acquire knowledge from outside the market process. In other words, while firms may have advantages over governments in some kinds of knowledge acquisition, governments may have the edge in certain other kinds.

However, we have to deal with a world in which the strength of these objections is not accepted, and where belief in the knowledge superiority of successful firms over governments has become an unchallengeable ideology, to the extent that chronic lack of self-confidence has affected public authorities at all levels, as we saw in chapter 2. To sustain their self-respect and give themselves any legitimacy at all, they try to make themselves as much like private firms as possible (e.g. through internal marketization), by bringing in expertise, consultants and actual service delivery from the private sector, and by privatizing and generally exposing as much of government (or former government) services as possible to the judgement of the financial markets. Nineteenth-century distinctions between the ethic of public service and that of private profit-making business are necessarily cast aside in such a process, and old inhibitions are rejected as outmoded. If the wisdom of firms is always superior to that of government, the idea of a proper limit of business influence on government becomes absurd.

This process becomes self-fulfilling. As government contracts out an increasing range of its activities, its employees really do lose competence in the areas being covered by the contractors, areas within which public servants have until now had unrivalled expertise. As they become mere brokers between public principals and private agents, so professional and technical knowledge pass to the latter. Before long it will become a serious argument in favour of private contractors that only they have the relevant expertise.

In the process of trying to make themselves as similar as possible to private firms, public authorities also have to divest themselves of an intrinsic aspect of their role: the fact that they are authorities. It should be noted that this loss does not extend to the political centre of national government itself. In fact, far from achieving the disappearance of state power dreamed of by libertarians, the privatizing state concentrates political power into the ellipse: a tight central nucleus, which deals predominantly with its peer elites in private business. This happens in the following way. Lower and intermediate authorities, in particular local government, have to transform their activities into the purchaser/provider model given by the market. The political authority role is therefore sucked out of them and is pulled to the centre. Central government also privatizes many of its own functions to consultants and suppliers of various kinds. But there is an irreducible political core which constitutes the elected part of capitalist national democracy, which cannot be sold off (though it can be compromised to lobbyists), and which wields the ultimate authority, at least over decisions how and whether to privatize and contract out. This core becomes ever smaller as privatization progresses, but it cannot be eliminated altogether without a collapse of the concept of both the state and democracy. The more that there is privatization and a marketization model for public-service delivery, particularly at local level, the more a Jacobin model of centralized democracy and a citizenship without intermediate levels of political action has to be imposed.

The loss of citizenship capacity

There are major problems in all this for the democratic rights of citizenship. Freedland (2001) has drawn attention to the triangular relationship: government, citizen, privatized supplier of services. The citizen has a link, through the democratic electoral and political system, to government (national or local). Government has a link, through the law of contract, with the privatized supplier. But the citizen has no link, neither of market nor of citizenship, to the supplier, and, following privatization, can no longer raise questions of service delivery with government, because it has contracted such delivery away. As a result the public service has become a post-democratic one: henceforth government is responsible to the *demos* only for broad policy, not for detailed implementation.

Freedland wrote before the various British railway crises of 2000–2, which demonstrated a further aspect: the sub-contracting chain. Following either privatization or contracting out, firms further sub-contract elements of their task, and the service moves even further away from citizens' reach. One of the main difficulties in establishing responsibility for railway failure has been the capacity of different sub-contractors in an ever-lengthening chain to lose responsibility in the legal labyrinth of contract terms which links them. A question over service delivery can be untangled only, if at all, in complex litigation.

There are therefore major risks in following the con-tracting-out route. However, governments will increasingly balance these against certain new tempting attractions. In trying to distance itself from service delivery through lengthy contract chains, government is imitating a discov-ery of the really smart firms of the 1990s that was dis-cussed in chapter 2: get rid of the core business itself! The firm can then concentrate on the sole task of developing its brand image with the use of advertising techniques rather than product quality. How much easier would the work of governments be if they needed to cultivate only their brand and image, and were not held to account for the actual quality of their policy products. Such processes clearly undermine the quality of democracy.

This leads us in turn to the final answer to the puzzle of what it is that private firms might offer which cannot be provided from within the public service itself: presenta-tion. Politicians themselves, although they are part of the public sector, inhabit a world far closer to that of the private sector, as they are constantly having to sell themselves and increasingly do so through branding and packaging. They see the value of this distinctive contribution of the private sector far more than they do that of the dour purveyors of health treatments and school lessons. And, more important, they know that the growth of the presentation approach within these services could remove the public gaze from their actual quality and focus it on the advertising and marketing schemes that private firms bring with them. In a fully spun political world, health, education and the rest would continue to be central to politics, but to a politics of branding, just as Coca-Cola ads refer somewhere to a drink. They would figure as sources of image association, not as items of substantive business. Electoral competition would continue to be intense and creative, as rival parties sought to associate themselves with the more winning imagery – but it would be a competition that the parties could keep under control.

Governments and parties cannot fully enter this ideal world until delivery of the education and health services and the rest of the welfare state have been sub-contracted to elongated supply chains of private firms, so that government is no more responsible for their production than Nike is for making the shoes it brands. If one runs this scenario through the Freedland triangle, one sees that citizens lose virtually all capacity to translate their concerns into political action. Elections become games around brands, rather than opportunities for citizens to talk back to politicians about the quality of services. Extreme though this might seem, it is only an extension of a process with which we have become so familiar that we no longer even notice it: the approximation of the democratic electoral process, the highest expression of citizenship rights, to a marketing campaign based quite openly on the manipulative techniques used to sell products.

6

Conclusions:
Where Do We Go From Here?

I have tried to show in the preceding discussions how the fundamental cause of democratic decline in contemporary politics is the major imbalance now developing between the role of corporate interests and those of virtually all other groups. Taken alongside the inevitable entropy of democracy, this is leading to politics once again becoming an affair of closed elites, as it was in pre-democratic times. The distortions operate at a number of levels: sometimes as external pressures exercised on governments; sometimes through internal changes within the priorities of government itself; sometimes within the very structure of political parties.

These changes are so powerful and widespread that it is impossible to see any major reversal of them. However, actions to try to shift contemporary politics partly away from the inexorable drift towards post-democracy are possible and can be propounded at three levels: policies to tackle the growing dominance of the corporate elite; policies for the reform of political practice as such; and actions available to concerned citizens themselves.

Dealing with corporate domination

The growing political power of the firm remains the fundamental change lying behind the advance of post-democracy. Among earlier generations of radicals this sentence would have been the cue for proposals for the abolition of capitalism. This is no longer viable. While enthusiasm for the capitalist mode of production has recently been taken to excess (namely the cases of privatized railways, water supply and air traffic control), no-one has yet found an effective alternative to the capitalist firm for process and product innovation and for customer responsiveness where most goods and services are concerned. The search must therefore be for ways of retaining the dynamism and enterprise of capitalism while preventing firms and their executives from exercising power to a degree incompatible with democracy. The currently fashionable reply to that proposition is that it is impossible: once we start regulating and restraining capitalist behaviour we rob it of its dynamism.

This is the bluff that the political world is afraid to call. At other times and places democracy has depended on the capacity of politicians to reduce the political power of business interests (or the military, or the church), while at the same time sustaining their effectiveness as a wealth-creating (fighting, moral) force. These balances have to be found if democracy is to thrive. Such a compromise was worked out between democracy and national manufacturing capitalism in the mid-twentieth century. Today it is global financial capitalism that has to be brought to terms.

But to ask for this at the global level at the present time is to cry for the moon. The framework of international governance established through the World Trade

Organization, the Organization for Economic Co-operation and Development, the International Monetary Fund and (for Europeans) the European Union is currently moving in the opposite direction. Virtually all measures of international economic 'reform' and liberalization involve breaking down barriers to corporate freedom. In a paradox very familiar from capitalist economic history, although the guiding theory is the achievement of near-perfect markets, in practice trade liberalization without regulation serves the interests of the biggest corporations. This creates oligopolies rather than free markets. Most of those originate in the USA, the world's sole super-power, and they can therefore add the government of that country to their lobbying strength within international organizations. And the US government is more committed to corporate freedom than most others. Areas of policy previously recognized as exceptions from free trade policies, such as health or aid to poor countries, are now being challenged by the US government, as in the losing struggles of the EU to protect European consumers from various chemical additives in US meat or to sustain its promises to Caribbean banana producers.

Throughout the 1990s Europeans, Japanese and others were told that the Anglo-American model of corporate governance and economic regulation was superior to their own. Its system of rules provided for transparency of behaviour by corporate management, in the first instance because of the powerful role played by shareholder interests in these neo-liberal economies. But we were also told that such transparency provided greater protection for the general public than did closer forms of state or associational regulation common elsewhere. Thus the interests of shareholders could be seen as equivalent to the public interest. Coming at a time when larger numbers of people were becoming shareholders in a small way, this seemed to provide a final answer to all leftist complaints that the capitalist economy required some external regulation and control.

The current wave of US accountancy scandals may force a revision of this view. Of course, all systems produce their scandals and malpractices. What was significant here, however, was the major failure of precisely the system of regulation that was supposed to provide the transparency that made the Anglo-American system so superior. As we have noted, in the lax, corporate-friendly public regulatory framework, the task of regulating the honesty of management was delegated to accountancy firms who were also permitted to sell other business services to the same managements whom they were supposed to be monitoring in shareholders' interests. And both these accountancy firms and the businesses with which they entered such a relationship are prominent in forming the new political ellipses described in chapter 4.

During 2002, the US government had imposed new tariffs and quotas on the import of steel, in clear violation of international treaties, in order to protect its own steel industry. This has considerably weakened the image of the US economy as one demonstrating the virtues of free trade against industrial policy. The time is ripe for a counter-attack on the Anglo-American model by all those who were cowed by the apparent superiority of its shareholder model of regulation during the 1990s. In particular it is time for the European Union to be less concerned with simple US imitation.

In itself the EU is hardly a shining example of democracy. Although the original European Economic Community came into existence during the high period of post-war democracy, it was itself conceived as a technocratic institution. Its internal democracy has been developed since the 1980s, a time when post-democratic approaches to governance have been dominant among elites. This democracy is therefore thin and cautious. These elements, together with the fact that most national governments have been concerned to ensure that European democracy is in no position to rival that of nation states, have produced extremely weak parliamentary structures, cut off from the real life of most of the population. This situation may improve as time passes. At least an elected parliament has been established, and the European Commission is constructing extensive relations with interest organizations within the nation states as well as in Brussels. However, the main role that the EU could play in democratization is at a different level. Merely by clearly asserting its own presence and some distinctive approaches, it can challenge the US dominance which will otherwise become totally hegemonic, and therefore eliminate alternatives and possibilities of choice – absolute minima for any democracy.

There is also scope for counter-attack on business dominance at a national level. The most urgent question here is reducing the overwhelming dominance that business interests have acquired within government through the various different processes identified in chapters 2 and 5. Indeed, achieving this within a large number of individual states is a precondition for any international action.

According to the neo-liberal ideology within whose terms virtually all governments today operate, these problems are resolved by establishing a proper market economy. It is argued that governments and business interests became too closely related under the old Keynesian and corporatist forms of social democratic economy. Once free markets rule, government knows and accepts its restricted role of setting the basic legal framework; and firms, knowing that government no longer intervenes in the economy, keep out of politics. If the past twenty years have taught us anything it is the error of this formulation. This is not only because the contracting out of public services – a policy commended by the ideology – requires close and continuing interaction between government officials and firms. More generally and subtly, once government is seen as essentially incompetent and firms as uniquely competent, as neo-liberal ideology implies, governments come under pressure to give over to firms and corporate leaders ever more control over public business. Far from clarifying the boundary between government and business, neo-liberalism has mixed them up in manifold new ways – but all within the former territory reserved to government.

Tackling the ensuing confusion of functions and temptations to corruption requires action at several levels. New rules are required to prevent, or at least very closely to regulate, flows of money and personnel between parties, circles of advisers and corporate lobbies. Relations between corporate donors, on the one hand, and public servants, public spending criteria and public policy-making, on the other, need to be clarified and codified. The concept of public service as a field of *sui generis* ethics and purposes needs to be re-established. It is instructive to reflect that the Victorian British elite, archetypal capitalists as they often were, developed and enforced a profound understanding of what distinguished public service from private profit-making, without at all opposing the proper functions of the latter. The particular rules they devised may well require radical amendment in a period when understanding of how large organizations can work has advanced far beyond the model of the classic bureaucracy; but the current orthodoxy – which simply maintains that the public service has 'a lot to learn' from private business – must be improved upon.

Research is required into the lessons – both positive and negative – which are now available to us following a number of years of penetration of public services by the private sector. What is the balance of improved efficiency against distorted goals? Given that business leaders today are invited to exercise influence, through donations and sponsorship, in public areas outside the fields of their business competence, do they confront professional practice simply with commercial judgement, or with chances to display personal idiosyncrasy, and if so, what are the consequences?

The citizens' dilemma

This task of researching and rethinking the political place of firms and their leading executives is one in which many can share. So is the formulation of new legal codes of conduct to bring global business behaviour within a framework of compromise with other social interests and concerns. But to whom is all this earnest activity addressed? Normally, of course, the main answer would be organs of government, but a major theme of this book has been the way in which governmental and party policy-making machinery, even of left-of-centre parties, has itself become endogenous to the problem of the power of the corporate elite. The above call for research into the effects of the role of the private sector within public services shows this. Who is to carry out such research? Government itself is today most likely to call upon private consultancy firms to do this, themselves leading examples of the problem. True to the image of active, positive citizens which I outlined as being the lifeblood of maximalist democracy in chapter 1, I therefore wish to end not by appealing to the political class itself to improve the quality of our democracy, but by asking what we ourselves need to do to have these issues placed on the real political agenda in the first place.

The logic of the arguments in this book seems to lead to alarmingly contradictory conclusions. On the one hand, it would seem that in post-democratic society we can no longer take for granted the commitment of particular parties to particular causes. This would lead to the conclusion that we should turn our backs on the party fight and devote our energies to cause organizations that we know will continue to press the issues about which we care. On the other hand we have also seen that the fragmentation of political action into a mass of causes and lobbies provides systematic advantages to the rich and powerful far greater than did a more party-dominated politics, where parties stood for relatively clear social constituencies. From this perspective, to desert party for cause group is only to conspire further in the triumph of post-democracy. However, again, to cling to the old model of the monolithic party is to sink into nostalgia for an irretrievable past.

Some observers connected with the search for a Third Way in politics, avoiding what they see as the cumbersome institutions of the recent past, are far more sanguine at the prospect of the replacement of big party organizations by more flexible and less conventionally 'political' structures. Leading examples are Anthony Giddens in *The Third Way* (1998) and Geoff Mulgan in *Politics in an Antipolitical Age* (1994). However, it is striking that neither of these authors regards capitalism as problematic, or sees major blocs of corporate power as at all fundamental to the dilemmas of contemporary society.

There are better ways of reconciling the contradiction between flexible new movements and solid old parties than by pretending that problems which can be confronted only by the latter no longer exist. Party remains fundamental to the avoidance of the anti-egalitarian tendencies of post-democracy. But we cannot rest content with working for our political goals solely by doing so *through* a party. We also have to work *on* a party from outside by assisting those causes that will sustain pressure on it. Parties which are not under pressure from causes will stay rooted in the post-democratic world of corporate lobbying; causes which try to act without reference to building strong parties will find themselves dwarfed by the corporate lobbies. We need to keep the two apparently contrasting forms of action – cause movements and parties – in relation to each other.

The continuing relevance of parties and elections

Politicians in many countries are becoming alarmed at growing voter apathy and declining membership in parties. This is the interesting paradox of the political class. It wants as much as possible to exclude the mass of citizens from becoming actively involved in probing its secrets, organizing oppositional activities, disturbing the tight control exercised by the politico-business ellipse. But it desperately wants us to offer passive support; it dreads the possibility that we might lose interest in its activities, fail to vote for it, give no money to its parties, ignore it. The solution it sees is to find means of encouraging the maximum level of minimal participation. If it is worried about voter apathy, it thinks about extending the opening hours of polling stations, or of enabling voting by telephone or Internet. If it is worried about declining party membership, it runs marketing campaigns to encourage supporters to take out membership subscriptions, but it does little to ensure that membership is an attractive and worthwhile activity.

The concerned egalitarian citizen will take a different approach to the same paradox, seeing the political elite's dependence on limited mass participation as a chance to find maximal opportunities for such engagement. Philippe Schmitter (2002) has made a number of highly imaginative and adventurous proposals for strengthening substantive participation, which address this issue far more effectively than the standard themes that emerge from established political organizations. For example, instead of the state funding of political parties commonly used in many European countries, where the money is divided among parties according to the outcome of the last general election, Schmitter proposes a direct democracy approach. A small fixed sum of every citizen's annual tax liability would be assigned to a political party chosen yearly by the citizen him- or herself; he proposes a similar approach to the funding of pressure groups and interest associations.

Even more radically, he proposes the institution of a citizens' assembly: a combination of ancient Greek democracy, the concept of jury service used in the law courts of Anglophone countries, and contemporary Swiss direct democracy. A month-long assembly of randomly selected citizens would review a small number of draft bills assigned to it by minorities (say one third) of regular members of parliament. The assembly would have the right to pass the bills into law or reject them. Clearly steps would need to be taken to ensure that powerful lobbies were unable to pressurize assembly members in a particular direction. But it, and the party funding proposal, have the merit of bringing ordinary people directly into political action and choice outside the framework of merely casting a ballot.

The citizens' assembly proposal would have particular value if extended to lower levels of regional and local government, as potentially vast numbers of citizens would in time have participated in such assemblies and might carry with them a legacy of political involvement, at least of understanding. In general there is potentially considerable scope for evading the problems of post-democracy at local level, because of the continuing role there of ordinary activists and the reduced presence of the ellipse. This gives a further reason in addition to those considered in chapter 5 to be worried at the current trend to privatize local public services and to reduce local government to a contracting agent, as these reduce the role of local political actors within the lives and decision-making processes of their communities. Given the greater accessibility and ease of participation in formal politics at local levels, democrats should be seeking to strengthen the role of local and regional politics, to advance the cause of decentralization, and to protect and enlarge the scope of the citizenship services for which local government is responsible.

Support for cause movements cannot replace the political party. However, this is not an argument for party loyalty. The more stubbornly loyal its core supporters, the more a party leadership can take them for granted and concentrate on responding to the powerful pressures being exercised upon it through the policy ellipse. In such a situation party members' strength grows as their support becomes conditional, and as this fact is made explicit and tangible. Egalitarians must therefore learn to risk a robust approach appropriate to post-democratic citizens, rewarding their party when it acts favourably and punishing it when it does not. For example, trade unions in the UK have recently started to divide their financial support among a number of cause organizations relevant to their members, rather than devote all to the Labour Party, as they did for many years. This follows that party's continuing neglect of their concerns.

But for this to be a progressive move, unions themselves need to be sure to be representing general and widespread social concerns, as they could reasonably claim to have done for much of the twentieth century, when they moved beyond representing skilled workers only to represent the mass of relatively under-privileged manual workers. Today they are going through their own parabola as a result of the changes in occupational structure described above, in danger of returning to caring for relatively privileged groups of those securely employed in manufacturing and public services, sometimes at the expense of those in new and in particular insecure sectors. German unions, for instance, continue to represent very intelligently the interests of standard male workers in manufacturing industry, but, precisely because they do that job so well, they have been reluctant to take an interest in the distinctive problems of women workers, workers with atypical contracts or those in newer services sectors. Elsewhere – for example in Italy – some unions today have particularly high proportions of retired persons among their members, and are therefore likely to represent their interests rather than those of current employees. This can be particularly important when the high cost of pension schemes raises social insurance charges and thus acts as a disincentive to job creation.

If unions become trapped into such positions, they become vulnerable to attack from opponents and prevent the construction of new solidarities among different sections of the new workforce. As discussed in chapter 3, problems of employment remain of enormous importance to people's lives, and the shaping of a political agenda around these remains central to the possibility of attracting ordinary people to see significance in politics and to discover new collective identities. The entry of so many women into the workforce makes working life relevant to a larger proportion of citizens than in the high period of class politics. These potentialities of the mainstream political system require politically alert and innovative unions. Unions are in a difficult position here, being largely victims of a particular pattern of occupational change. But, if they so choose, they are in a position to act strategically to avoid the trap. The Italian unions showed this in the early 1990s, when their support for the general public-interest policy of Italy's entry into the single European currency led them to accept a major pensions reform.

Mobilizing new identities

However far post-democracy advances, it is unlikely that it will exhaust the capacity for new social identities to form, to become aware of their outsider status in the political system, and to make both noisy and articulate demands for admission, disrupting the stage-managed and slogan-ridden world of conventional post-democratic electoral politics. We have already seen how feminist movements have provided very recent, very major instances of this. Ecological movements provide others. This constant scope for new disruptive creativity within the *demos* gives egalitarian democrats their main hope for the future.

Both feminist and ecological movements followed the classic pattern of past mobilizations (Della Porta and Diani 1999; Eder 1993; Pizzorno 1977). An identity develops and is defined by various vanguard groups; frustrated by political exclusion, some of these become extreme and possibly violent. But if the cause has any resonance with a wider public, it spreads; its concerns filter into the language and thoughts of ordinary people who are not normally caught up in causes. It becomes incoherent and internally contradictory. The world of official politics is taken by surprise, finds the movement unmanageable and attacks it as undemocratic; more articulate demands are formulated; the elite finds means of responding to these; the movement has entered politics, and begins to experience a mixed pattern of victories and defeats.

Now, to accept this point is to invert the perspective usually adopted by the political world of what constitutes democracy and what its negation. Faced with difficult and disruptive new demands, elected politicians have one response: they themselves constitute the embodiment of democratic choice; we have our chance to make that choice in elections every few years; anyone who causes trouble in seeking major change at other times or in other ways is therefore attacking democracy itself. (Curiously, they never mention the pressures for policy favours from business interests to which they are permanently subject, but we have said enough about that.) From this perspective my creatively troublesome *demos* is an anti-democratic mob.

We must be careful here. At the present time, in addition to feminist and ecological movements, the groups that are seeking attention include violent animal rights campaigns, the extreme components of the 'no-global' anti-capitalism campaign, racist organizations and various incipiently lynching anti-criminal movements. It is a mistake to be gleeful every time that the political class has its feathers badly ruffled: that way lies the absurd and dangerous welcome that many were tempted to give to Jörg Haider in Austria, Pim Fortuyn in the Netherlands and their populist and racist counterparts in Belgium, France, Denmark and elsewhere. We must always discriminate, and at two levels. First is the decision whether to welcome the emergence of a particular new movement as compatible with democracy, contributing to civic vigour and preventing politics from disappearing into a manipulative game among elites. Second is the decision whether personally to support, oppose or remain indifferent to its objectives.

There is a difference in what we welcome as democrats and what we actually support as egalitarian democrats. But I would insist that it is at these points that we make our discriminations and judgements, not at the prior point on which the political class invites us to concentrate, which would have us accept as democratic only those groups and issues already fully processed by their machines. Behind the image of destructive negativism which haunts the new anti-globalization movement lie in fact many constructive and innovative ideas and groups, concerned not with violence and opposing economic change, but seriously seeking out new forms of democracy and forms of inter-nationalism that do not exploit the people of the third world. These movements are 'new global' rather than 'no-global', in the words of one of their keenest and most perceptive observers (Della Porta 2003). Everyone con-cerned for the future of not only democracy but also sustainable human life itself needs to listen with a discrim-inating ear to what is emerging here.

The mobilizing issues which will nourish the future development of the left and centre – in particular cam-paigns against the consequences of uncontrolled global capitalism – are in danger of being neglected or rejected by some reformist movements. The initiative in articulat-ing new concerns is therefore shifting to the far right. If this continues, not only will the right manage to define and orchestrate the only forms of expressed discontent to achieve political salience, but also it will be able falsely to represent itself as living outside the closed world of the political class, speaking directly from and to the people, and shaping identities from the shapeless 'middle mass' of contemporary electorates. Racist and populist movements have already acquired a new role and respectability in the politics of contemporary Western European countries. This growing ascendancy will not be contested by moderate parties trying to siphon off votes from far right parties by imitating their hostility to immigrants and ethnic minorities, though this is the easy temptation to which most of them are submitting. Nor will it be contested solely by trying to fight racism. There must also be alternative forms of movement and articulation of discontent, which rival and challenge those orchestrated by the populists. The far right speaks of the problems of globalization or *mondialisation*, but then focuses these problems on the persons of immigrants, who are themselves globalization's biggest victims, and not the cause of the problems it presents. The discontents need to be refocused on the true causes of the problems: the large corporations and exclusive profit-seeking behaviour that are destroying communities and creating instability the world over.

Nor will populism be contested by trying to move 'beyond' identity politics to a Third Way political appeal which tries to evade the very idea of identity. As Pizzorno (1993, 2000) has argued, political parties that claim to represent masses of people need to do so by articulating an identity for those people, something that defines the concerns and interests of the group so defined. One needs to point out that there is nothing essential in such identities, and that much depends on the mobilizing skill of the political entrepreneurs who work at them. Constructed though identities are, the consequences of successful identity formation are very real indeed. If people are encouraged to form their identity on the basis of opposition to certain racial groups, or to public employees, and are encouraged to define their frustrations and discontents as having been caused primarily by these groups, politics will become focused on these targets, and other issues will be ignored. There are many potential identities being formed among the new types of occupation and the new forms of family life being created by the post-industrial economy.

Their lack of formation and mobilization reflects not any lack of need of representation, but a refusal of existing organizations to articulate those identities, and the difficulty of new organizations to emerge within the controlled, crowded spaces of contemporary politics. For organizations of the political left in particular, denial of the role of identity formation among those outside narrow elite circles constitutes a denial of their own fundamental sources of vitality (Pizzorno 2000: 201).

Established parties themselves may feel that it is too risky for them to become involved in new social movements. Of many attempts to articulate identities, most will fail and only a few will succeed. An established party risks sinking all its resources in a speculative attempt to create a particular focus of political concern, only to discover that it does not work. Large corporations often avoid risky investments, but watch out for which of a large number of small firms happens on a strong idea; they then take over those firms. Similarly, there needs to be an open market of contest for defining political identities which lies outside but close to the oligopolistic arena of the established parties. Individuals associated with those parties need to involve themselves in such activities if eventually successful ones are to be embraced. Democratic politics therefore needs a vigorous, chaotic, noisy context of movements and groups. They are the seedbeds of future democratic vitality.

There were important examples of this during 2002 and 2003 in Italy, as the Berlusconi government increasingly and blatantly legislated to protect the past, present and future business practices of its leaders from the scrutiny of financial and criminal law. This generated a large, broadly based mass movement of protest expressing disgust, capable of mobilizing very large public demonstrations and processions, largely organized outside the scope of the centre-left parties, which were seen to have failed adequately to express the contempt and concern of many citizens – and themselves to have been too close to similar politico-business networks. The parties – though not the Confederazione Generale Italiana del Lavoro, the main trade union confederation – were at first nervous about taking strong actions of this kind, fearing that contemporary populations would be more hostile to politicians who marched in the streets to protest at corruption than they would be to those suspected of the corruption.

Protests in favour of the integrity of the justice system and for business probity are hardly radical; in the eighteenth century they were the minimal demands considered necessary for the capitalist economy to operate efficiently. That they are in twenty-first-century Italy the demands that define an extra-parliamentary opposition is further evidence of the problematic state of Italian democracy. But the Italian case does demonstrate certain generalizable points. First, in contrast with the US electorate after the 2000 presidential election, many Italians are demonstrating that ordinary people can be encouraged to care about the probity of their political system; they are not all blasé and sunk in cynicism. Second, it is possible to organize major movements without the help of the political class. Third, it may be better that the political class of the centre-left remains on the sidelines and does not become closely associated with new movements, because its aversion to the risk of unpopularity leads it to inhibit any radical gestures. Finally, and most important, we can learn that is not a fact of nature that people care more about immigrants moving to their town than they do about any issues embarrassing to the political right. The withdrawal of genetically modified foods from supermarkets in most European countries in response to widespread consumer concern was a more general example. This insight might well be extended to, say, the stress of increasingly precarious working conditions. It is possible for such campaigns to be as popular as those of the far right, but the campaigns have to be waged, interests have to be defined and causes of discontents identified. They will not emerge automatically.

Conclusion

So have egalitarian democrats come full circle to where they were in the late nineteenth century, lobbying the political elites of various parties without having a party to call their own? No; because we are moving through a parabola and not a circle. We have moved along its length to a new historical point, and we carry a history of organization building and achievement that we must not squander. It is the duality of this situation that teaches us our apparently contradictory lessons. First, stay alert to the potentialities of new movements which may at first seem difficult to understand, because they may be the bearers of democracy's future vitality. Second, work through the lobbies of established and new cause organizations, because post-democratic politics works through lobbies. Even if the causes supported by egalitarians are always weaker there than those of the large corporations, they are weaker still if they stay out of the lobby. And, third, work, critically and conditionally, through parties, because none of their post-democratic substitutes can replace their potential capacity for carrying through egalitarian policies.

Meanwhile, however, we know that on many of the major issues which currently confront us, the claims made by global firms that they will not be able to operate profitably unless freed from regulation and subordination to criteria of welfare and redistribution will continue to trump all polite democratic debate. This was also the main burden of capitalism's political stance in the nineteenth and early twentieth centuries. It was forced to make what in retrospect now seems to have been a temporary compromise by a complicated set of forces: its own long-term inability to secure economic stability; the unmanageable violence sometimes caused by both its own flirtations with fascism and its confrontations with communism; largely non-violent but still disruptive struggles against trade unions; the sheer inefficiency of neglected social infrastructure; and the growing plausibility of social democratic parties and policy alternatives.

How essential were the reality and fears of chaos and disruption within that complex general equation? It is impossible to pretend that they played no part. Both the social compromise of the mid-twentieth century and the associated interlude of relatively maximal democracy, epitomes of peacefulness and order though they were in themselves, were forged in a crucible that included turmoil. It is necessary to remember this, as we condemn sections among the no-global demonstrators for their violence, their anarchism and their negative lack of viable alternatives to the capitalist economy. We must ask ourselves: without a massive escalation of truly disruptive actions of the kind that those demonstrators advocate, will anything reverse the profit calculations of global capital enough to bring its representatives to the bargaining table, to force an end to child slavery and other forms of labour degradation, to the production of levels of pollution that are now visibly destroying our atmosphere, to the wasteful use of non-renewable resources, to growing extremes of wealth and poverty both within and between nations? These are the questions that most challenge the health of contemporary democracy.

References

Almond, G.A. and Verba, S. 1963, *The Civic Culture: Political Attitudes and Democracy in Five Nations*. Princeton, NJ: Princeton University Press.

Bagnasco, A. 1999, 'Teoria del capitale sociale e *political economy* comparata', *Stato e Mercato* 57: 351–72.

Castells, M. 1996, *The Rise of Network Society*. Oxford: Blackwell.

Corbett, J. and Jenkinson, T. 1996, 'The Financing of Industry, 1970–1989: An International Comparison', *Journal of the Japanese and International Economies* 10: 71.

Crick, B. 1980, *George Orwell: A Life*. London: Secker and Warburg.

Crouch, C. 1999a, *Social Change in Western Europe*. Oxford: Oxford University Press.

Crouch, C. 1999b, 'The Parabola of Working Class Politics', in A. Gamble and T. Wright (eds), *The New Social Democracy*. Oxford: Blackwell.

Dahl, R.A. 1989, *Democracy and its Critics*. New Haven: Yale University Press.

Davies, G. and Graham, A. 1997, *Broadcasting, Society and Policy in the Multimedia Age*. Luton: University of Luton.

Della Porta, D. 2000, *Political Parties and Corruption: 17 Hypotheses on the Interactions between Parties and Corruption*. Working Paper RSC 2000/60. Florence: European University Institute.

Della Porta, D. 2003, *I new global*. Bologna: Il Mulino.

Della Porta, D. and Diani, M. 1999, *Social Movements: An Introduction*. Oxford: Blackwell.

Della Porta, D. and Mény, Y. (eds) 1995, *Démocratie et corruption en Europe*. Paris: La Découverte.

Della Porta, D. and Vannucci, A. 1999, *Corrupt Exchanges: Actors, Resources, and Mechanisms of Political Corruption*. New York: Aldine de Gruyter.

Dore, R. 2000, *Stock Market Capitalism: Welfare Capitalism: Japan and Germany versus the Anglo-Saxons*. Oxford: Oxford University Press.

Eder, K. 1993, *The New Politics of Class: Social Movements and Cultural Dynamics in Advanced Societies*. London: Sage Publications.

Freedland, M.R, 2001, 'The Marketization of Public Services', in C. Crouch, K. Eder and D. Tambini (eds), *Citizenship, Markets and the State*. Oxford: Clarendon Press.

Giddens, A. 1998, *The Third Way*. Cambridge: Polity.

Hardin, R. 2000, 'The Public Trust', in S.J. Pharr and R.D. Putnam (eds), *Disaffected Democracies: What's Troubling the Trilateral Countries?* (2000), Princeton, NJ: Princeton University Press.

Hatcher, R. 2000, 'Getting down to Business'. Paper presented at conference on 'Privatisierung des Bildungsbereichs', University of Hamburg.

Hirschman, A.O. 1970, *Exit, Voice, and Loyalty: Responses to Decline in Firms, Organizations, and States*. Cambridge, Mass.: Harvard University Press.

King, D.S. 1995, *Actively Seeking Work? The Politics of Unemployment and Welfare Policy in the United States and Great Britain*. Chicago: University of Chicago Press.

Kiser, E. and Laing, A.M. 2001, 'Have We Overestimated the Effects of Neoliberalism and Globalization? Some Speculations on the Anomalous Stability of Taxes on Business', in J.L. Campbell and O.K. Pedersen (eds), *The Rise of Neoliberalism and Institutional Analysis*. Princeton, NJ: Princeton University Press.

Klein, N. 2000, *No Logo: No Space, No Choice, No Jobs: Taking Aim at the Brand Bullies*. London: Flamingo.

Lindblom, C.E. 1977, *Politics and Markets: The World's Political Economic Systems*. New York: Basic Books.

Maravall, J.M. 1997: *Regimes, Politics and Markets: Democratization and Economic Change in Southern and Eastern Europe*. Oxford: Oxford University Press.

Marshall, T.H. 1963, *Sociology at the Crossroads and Other Essays*. London: Routledge and Kegan Paul.

Mulgan, G. 1994, *Politics in an Antipolitical Age*. Cambridge: Polity.

Mulgan, G. (ed.) 1997, *Life after Politics: New Thinking for the Twenty-First Century*. London: Demos and Fontana.

Pharr, S.J. and Putnam, R.D. (eds) 2000, *Disaffected Democracies: What's Troubling the Trilateral Countries?* Princeton, NJ: Princeton University Press.

Pharr, S.J., Putnam, R.D. and Dalton, R. J. 2000, 'Introduction', in S.J. Pharr and R.D. Putnam (eds), *Disaffected Democracies: What's Troubling the Trilateral Countries?* Princeton, NJ: Princeton University Press.

Piselli, F. 1999, 'Capitale sociale: un concetto situazionale e dinamico', *Stato e Mercato* 57: 395–418.

Pizzorno, A. 1977, 'Scambio politico e identità collettiva nel conflitto di classe', in C. Crouch and A. Pizzorno (eds), *Conflitti in Europa: Lotte di Classe, Sindacati e Stato dopo il '68*. Milan: Etas Libri.

Pizzorno, A. 1993, *Le radici della politica assoluta e altri saggi*. Milan: Feltrinelli.

Pizzorno, A. 2000, 'Risposte e proposte', in D. Della Porta, M. Greco and A. Szakoczai A. (eds), *Identità, riconoscimento, scambio*. Rome: Laterza.

Price, D., Pollock, A. and Shaoul, J. 1999, 'How the World Trade Organization is Shaping Domestic Policies in Health Care', *The Lancet*, 354, 27 November: 1889–92.

Przeworski, A. and Meseguer Yebra, C. 2002, *Globalization and Democracy*. Working Paper 2002/183. Madrid: Instituto Juan March.

Putnam, R.D., with Leonardi, R. and Nanetti, R. 1993, *Making Democracy Work: Civic Traditions in Modern Italy*. Princeton, NJ: Princeton University Press.

Reich, R. 1991, *The Work of Nations: Preparing Ourselves for 21st Century Capitalism*. New York: Vintage Books.

Schmitter, P.C. (2002) 'A Sketch of What a "Post-Liberal" Democracy Might Look Like'. Unpublished manuscript. Florence: European University Institute.

Schmitter, P.C. and Brouwer, I. 1999, *Conceptualizing, Researching and Evaluating Democracy Promotion and Protection*. Working Paper SPS 1999/9. Florence: European University Institute.

Titmuss, R.M. 1970, *The Gift Relationship: From Human Blood to Social Policy*. London: Allen & Unwin.

Trigilia, C. 1999, 'Capitale sociale e sviluppo locale', *Stato e Mercato* 57: 419–40.

Van Kersbergen, K. 1996, *Social Capitalism: A Study of Christian Democracy and the Welfare State*. London: Routledge.

Visser, J. and Hemerijck, A. 1997, *A Dutch 'Miracle'*. Amsterdam: Amsterdam University Press.

Index